SHOOT-OUT IN CLEVELAND

BLACK MILITANTS AND THE POLICE:

A Report to the
National Commission on
the Causes and Prevention of
Violence

by
Louis H. Masotti
and
Jerome R. Corsi

May 1969

For sale by the Superintendent of Documents, U.S. Government Printing Office
Washington, D.C. 20402 - Price 75 cents

Official editions of publications of the National Commission on the Causes and Prevention of Violence may be freely used, duplicated or published, in whole or in part, except to the extent that, where expressly noted in the publications, they contain copyrighted materials reprinted by permission of the copyright holders. Photographs may have been copyrighted by the owners, and permission to reproduce may be required.

Library of Congress Catalog Card Number: 72-602071

STATEMENT ON THE STAFF STUDIES

The Commission was directed to "go as far as man's knowledge takes it" in searching for the causes of violence and means of prevention. These studies are reports to the Commission by independent scholars and lawyers who have served as directors of our staff task forces and study teams; they are not reports by the Commission itself. Publication of any of the reports should not be taken to imply endorsement of their contents by the Commission, or by any member of the Commission's staff, including the Executive Director and other staff officers not directly responsible for the preparation of the particular report. Both the credit and the responsibility for the reports lie in each case with the directors of the task forces and study teams. The Commission is making the reports available at this time as works of scholarship to be judged on their merits, so that the Commission as well as the public may have the benefit of both the reports and informed criticism and comment on their contents.

Dr. Milton S. Eisenhower, *Chairman*

30766

SHOOT-OUT IN CLEVELAND

Co-Directors

Louis H. Masotti
Jerome R. Corsi

Editorial Consultant

Anthony E. Neville

Pictorial Consultant

Judith Harkinson

Commission Staff Officers

Lloyd N. Cutler, *Executive Director*
Thomas D. Barr, *Deputy Director*
James F. Short, Jr., Marvin E. Wolfgang, *Co-Directors of Research*
James S. Campbell, *General Counsel*
William G. McDonald, *Administrative Office*
Joseph Laitin, *Director of Information*
Ronald A. Wolk, *Special Assistant to the Chairman*

National Commission on the Causes and Prevention of Violence

Dr. Milton S. Eisenhower, *Chairman*

PREFACE

From the earliest days of organization, the Chairman, Commissioners, and Executive Director of the National Commission on the Causes and Prevention of Violence recognized the importance of research in accomplishing the task of analyzing the many facets of violence in America. As a result of this recognition, the Commission has enjoyed the receptivity, encouragement, and cooperation of a large part of the scientific community in this country. Because of the assistance given in varying degrees by scores of scholars here and abroad, these Task Force reports represent some of the most elaborate work ever done on the major topics they cover.

The Commission was formed on June 10, 1968. By the end of the month, the Executive Director had gathered together a small cadre of capable young lawyers from various Federal agencies and law firms around the country. That group was later augmented by partners borrowed from some of the Nation's major law firms who served without compensation. Such a professional group can be assembled more quickly than university faculty because the latter are not accustomed to quick institutional shifts after making firm commitments of teaching or research at a particular locus. Moreover, the legal profession has long had a major and traditional role in Federal agencies and commissions.

In early July a group of 50 persons from the academic disciplines of sociology, psychology, psychiatry, political science, history, law, and biology were called together on short notice to discuss for 2 days how best the Commission and its staff might proceed to analyze violence. The enthusiastic response of these scientists came at a moment when our Nation was still suffering from the tragedy of Senator Kennedy's assassination.

It was clear from that meeting that the scholars were prepared to join research analysis and action, interpretation, and policy. They were eager to present to the American people the best available data, to bring reason to bear where myth had prevailed. They cautioned against simplistic solutions, but urged application of what is known in the service of sane policies for the benefit of the entire society.

Shortly thereafter the position of Director of Research was created. We assumed the role as a joint undertaking, with common responsibilities. Our function was to enlist social and other scientists to join the staff, to write papers, act as advisers or consultants, and engage in new research. The decentralized structure of the staff, which at its peak numbered 100, required research coordination to reduce duplication and to fill in gaps among the original seven separate Task Forces. In general, the plan was for each Task Force to have a pair of directors: one a social scientist, one a lawyer. In a number of instances, this formal structure bent before the necessities of available personnel but in almost every case the Task Force work program relied on both social scientists and lawyers for its successful completion. In addition to our work with the seven original Task Forces, we provided consultation for the work of the eighth "Investigative" Task Force, formed originally to investigate the disorders at the Democratic and Republican National Conventions and the civil strife in Cleveland during the summer of 1968 and eventually expanded to study campus disorders at several colleges and universities.

Throughout September and October and in December of 1968 the Commission held about 30 days of public hearings related expressly to each of the Task Force areas. About 100 witnesses testified, including many scholars, Government officials, corporate executives as well as militants and activists of various persuasions. In addition to the hearings, the Commission and the staff met privately with scores of persons, including college presidents, religious and youth leaders, and experts in such areas as the media, victim compensation, and firearms. The staff participated actively in structuring and conducting those hearings and conferences and in the questioning of witnesses.

As Research Directors, we participated in structuring the strategy of design for each Task Force, but we listened more than directed. We have known the delicate details of some of the statistical problems and computer runs. We have argued over philosophy and syntax; we have offered bibliographical and other resource materials, we have written portions of reports and copy edited others. In short, we know the enormous energy and devotion, the long hours and accelerated study that members of each Task Force have invested in their labors. In retrospect we are amazed at the high caliber and quantity of the material produced, much of which truly represents, the best in research and scholarship. About 150 separate papers and projects were involved in the work culminating in the Task Force reports. We feel less that we have orchestrated than that we have been members of the orchestra, and that together with the entire staff we have helped compose a repertoire of current knowledge about the enormously complex subject of this Commission.

That scholarly research is predominant in the work here presented is evident in the product. But we should like to emphasize that the roles which we occupied were not limited to scholarly inquiry. The Directors of Research were afforded an opportunity to participate in all Commission meetings. We engaged in discussions at the highest levels of decisionmaking, and had great freedom in the selection of scholars, in the control of research budgets, and in the direction and design of research. If this was not unique, it is at least an uncommon degree of prominence accorded research by a national commission.

There were three major levels to our research pursuit: (1) summarizing the state of our present knowledge and clarifying the lacunae where more or new research should be encouraged; (2) accelerating known ongoing research so as to make it available to the Task Forces; (3) undertaking new research projects within the limits of time and funds available. Coming from a university setting where the pace of research is more conducive to reflection and quiet hours analyzing data, we at first thought that completing much meaningful new research within a matter of months was most unlikely. But the need was matched by the talent and enthusiasm of the staff, and the Task Forces very early had begun enough new projects to launch a small university with a score of doctoral theses. It is well to remember also that in each volume here presented, the research reported is on full public display and thereby makes the staff more than usually accountable for their products.

One of the very rewarding aspects of these research undertakings has been the experience of minds trained in the law mingling and meshing, sometimes fiercely arguing, with other minds trained in behavioral science. The organizational structure and the substantive issues of each Task Force required members from both groups. Intuitive judgment and the logic of argument and organization blended, not always smoothly, with the methodology of science and statistical reasoning. Critical and analytical faculties were sharpened as theories confronted facts. The arrogance neither of ignorance nor of certainty could long endure the doubts and questions of interdisciplinary debate. Any sign of approaching the priestly pontification of scientism was quickly dispelled in the matrix of mutual criticism. Years required for the normal accumulation of experience were compressed into months of sharing ideas with others who had equally valid but differing perspectives. Because of this process, these volumes are much richer than they otherwise might have been.

Partly because of the freedom which the Commission gave to the Directors of Research and the Directors of each Task Force, and partly to retain the full integrity of the research work in publication, these reports of the Task Forces are in the posture of being submitted to and received by the Commission. These are volumes published under the authority of the Commission, but they do not necessarily represent the views or the conclusions of the Commission. The Commission is presently at work producing its own report, based in part on the materials presented to it by the Task Forces. Commission members have, of course, commented on earlier drafts of each Task Force, and have caused alterations by reason of the cogency of their remarks and insights. But the final responsibility for what is contained in these volumes rests fully and properly on the research staffs who labored on them.

In this connection, we should like to acknowledge the special leadership of the Chairman, Dr. Milton S. Eisenhower, in formulating and supporting the principle of research freedom and autonomy under which this work has been conducted.

We note, finally, that these volumes are in many respects incomplete and tentative. The urgency with which papers were prepared and then integrated into Task Force Reports rendered impossible the successive siftings of data and argument to which the typical academic article or volume is subjected. The reports have benefited greatly from the counsel of our colleagues on the Advisory Panel, and from much debate and revision from within the staff. It is our hope, that the total work effort of the Commission staff will be the source and subject of continued research by scholars in the several disciplines, as well as a useful resource for policymakers. We feel certain that public policy and the disciplines will benefit greatly from such further work.

*   *   *

To the Commission, and especially to its Chairman, for the opportunity they provided for complete research freedom, and to the staff for its prodigious and prolific work, we, who were intermediaries and servants to both, are most grateful.

James F. Short, Jr.   Marvin E. Wolfgang

Directors of Research

PREFACE 1

This report began to be compiled in the summer of 1968, even before the smoke had cleared from 5 days of racial violence in Cleveland. Two institutions shared our belief in the national significance of the events in Cleveland and generously underwrote the study: the Lemberg Center for the Study of Violence, Brandeis University, and the National Institute of Mental Health, Washington, D.C. In September, the National Commission on the Causes and Prevention of Violence, also recognizing the significance of these events, lent support to the study and urged that it be completed by November 15, 1968.

Hundreds of man-hours were invested in interviewing, research, writing, and in safeguarding accuracy and completeness as we rushed to meet the deadline. Of the more than 20 Civil Violence Research Center staff members and project consultants, four deserve our special commendation: Mrs. Robert Dickman, John Krause, Jr., Mrs. Yoram Papir, and Mrs. Robert Bauerlein. They performed innumerable and often overwhelming administrative, clerical, and intellectual tasks, tirelessly bearing the brunt of the pressure to finish the report. Ellen Cummings lent her legal expertise, and Timothy Armbruster and Mrs. Jeffrey Zerby their interpretive skills; Estelle Zannes, Lauren McKinsey, James Monhart, Robert Farlow, Kermit Allen, III, Forrester Lee, and Sharon Dougherty conducted more than 200 interviews that provided the raw material for large sections of the report. Julie Reinstein provided invaluable assistance in the office. Two of our colleagues were especially helpful: Prof. Jeffrey K. Hadden, who helped to initiate and design the project, and Prof. Charles McCaghy, who conducted several key interviews.

Many Clevelanders were exceedingly cooperative. Mayor Carl B. Stokes, the members of his cabinet and staff; Police Chief Michael Blackwell and some police officers; editors and reporters of both the electronic and printed news media; the leadership of Cleveland's black community; Fred (Ahmed) Evans and his attorney, Stanley Tolliver; members of Cleveland's City Council; businessmen of the Glenville area—all gave generously of their time and knowledge. Others were not cooperative, stating that they could not divulge information until after the trial of Fred Evans, the black militant who was indicted on seven counts of first-degree murder in connection with the racial disturbances. Some important records, such as the tapes of police radio calls during the nights of violence, were unobtainable.

A draft of the report was finished November 15, coincident with another report sponsored by the National Commission on Violence on the demonstrations in Chicago during the Democratic National Convention of 1968 (the Walker Report). While that report was published soon thereafter, this one was not. An important difference in the circumstances was that, in our case, the report narrated events for which a man was about to go on trial for his life. The Commission took the position that release of this report prior to the murder trial of Fred Evans (completed on May 12, 1969) would be improper because—

> . . . criminal trials of some of the alleged participants in the incidents which are the subject of the report were likely to begin in the near future. The Commission felt that the public interest would be as well served by postponing release of the report until after the trials, and this course of action would avoid any possible interference with the prosecution or defense of those cases.

The pros and cons of pretrial publicity have been the subject of much debate. The American Bar Association and the legal profession generally believe that publicity as to the details of events that may be relevant to the trial should be avoided, so that the jury can arrive at its decision solely on the basis of the evidence presented to it in the courtroom with full opportunity to consider the demeanor of witnesses and their responses under cross-examination. The Nation's media urge a more liberal standard in the name of the constitutional freedom of the press.

The balance between the constitutional right to a fair trial and the public's right to know is a difficult one to strike. It was the Commission's prerogative to decide this policy question as it did. Scholars might have decided it differently.

Even though the trial is now over and the verdict is in, it is still difficult for us to decide in our minds what effect prior publication would have had on the conduct of the trial and the judgment reached. Readers themselves can judge the fairness and objectivity of this report. We have not attempted, in this report, to pronounce judgments where none is warranted. Indeed, a frequent theme in this report is that many important questions have gone unanswered. What we have attempted is a coherent narrative of the events of the fateful evening of July 23, 1968, organizing the details to facilitate analysis, raising questions where they are warranted, and mirroring the shootout in Cleveland against the events that led up to it and those it precipitated. For jurors during the Evans trial, a picture of the events of July 23 emerged only through weeks of testimony, presented in no logical sequence and often interrupted by challenges, legal debates, conferences at the bench, recesses, and the other discontinuities that make criminal trials move slower than baseball games.

Whatever the wisdom of the Commission's decision (and it is now, in another sense, an "academic matter"), their reason for withholding this report from publication did not satisfy all critics. Among those inclined to see conspiracies where none exists (a disposition of extreme leftists as well as those on the far right), there were suspicions that the Commission was suppressing the report because it contained conclusions distasteful to the Establishment point of view. In Cleveland's black community, the rumor was afloat that the report was being rewritten at the Commission's direction to excise passages that would cast doubt on the guilt of Fred Evans. Neither suspicion had any basis in fact, since no one representing the Commission on Violence ever addressed a comment to us that in any way challenged the substance of our report.

We did not spend the period of forced silence idly, however. Those months gave us an opportunity all authors cherish: a chance to review the effort, improve it structurally, and sharpen the prose style. In this effort we had the invaluable editorial assistance of Anthony E. Neville, a professional writer. Gradually what had begun as a *report*, a document with no greater ambition than to be factual, thorough, and useful to a special audience, took on the aspects of a *book*, structured and phrased to inform the general public. When the trial of Fred Evans was over, we added an epilog discussing that event.

In a sense, however, this book is still incomplete. Fred Evans was convicted of first-degree murder by an all-white jury under an Ohio law that required no proof that he ever pulled a trigger. The effects of that verdict on the black community in Cleveland are not yet clear. Moreover, the circumstances that bred racial violence in Cleveland in the summer of 1968 have not changed significantly since then, and no one can say with confidence that it will not happen again. America itself has not changed in the ways that matter. It could happen again—anywhere.

L. H. M.
J. R. C.

Cleveland, Ohio
May 16, 1969

INTRODUCTION

On the evening of July 23, 1968, shots rang out on a narrow street in Cleveland's racially troubled East Side. Within minutes, a full-scale gun battle was raging between Cleveland police and black snipers. An hour and a half later, seven people lay dead; 15 others were wounded. Fifteen of the casualties were policemen.

For the next 5 days, violence flared in Glenville and other East Side neighborhoods. Arsonists heaved fire bombs into buildings; teenagers smashed store windows and led mobs in looting. The police lashed back, sometimes in blind fury. In the smoldering aftermath, 63 business establishments were counted damaged or destroyed. Property losses exceeded $2 million.

In human and dollar costs, the Glenville incident was not the most serious event in the recent tide of racial violence in America. But it differed sharply from the current pattern of violence in significant, instructive ways. Indeed, it established a new theme and an apparent escalation in the level of racial conflict in America.

Racial clashes have produced bloodshed and property damage before. Most recent outbreaks, like the Detroit riot of 1967, were initiated by blacks—itself a deviation from earlier patterns—but the hostility was directed toward property, not persons. (Sporadic sniper fire—less of it than originally believed—occurred during major disorders in 1967, but long after the violence had expressed itself in property damage.) The Glenville incident was different; it began as person-oriented violence, black and whites shooting at each other, snipers against cops. And apparently alone among major outbreaks of racial violence in American history, it ended in more white casualties than black.

Moreover, the Glenville incident occurred in the first major American city to have elected a Negro mayor and in a city that had been spared serious disorders during the volatile summer of 1967. Because of Carl B. Stokes' success in preventing violence after the assassination of Martin Luther King in April 1968, Clevelanders looked upon him as a positive guarantee against future racial disturbances in their city. Yet the violence occurred, and the Glenville incident raised disturbing questions for other American cities with increasing Negro populations that can expect to have Negro-led governments in the future.

Lastly, Mayor Stokes introduced a new technique for quenching the violence. At the urging of black leaders, he placed control of the troubled neighborhoods in their hands, barring white policemen, National Guardsmen, and white nonresidents from the area. After one night's trial, the policy was altered; police and National Guardsmen were brought into the area, chiefly to protect property. Born in controversy, carried out under complicating circumstances and with only partial success, the technique of "community control" during riots is still a matter of dispute as to its effectiveness.

Why did it happen, especially in Cleveland? Was the Glenville incident the result of a vast conspiracy to "get Whitey" or the sudden, unpremeditated act of a few individuals? Who is to blame? Will it happen again—in Cleveland or elsewhere?

CONTENTS

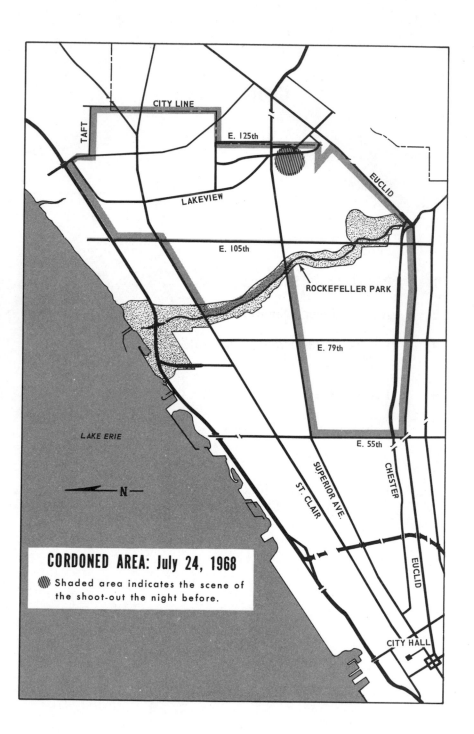

CITY LINE

TAFT

E. 125th

LAKEVIEW

EUCLID

E. 105th

ROCKEFELLER PARK

E. 79th

LAKE ERIE

N

E. 55th

SUPERIOR AVE.

ST. CLAIR

CHESTER

EUCLID

CITY HALL

CORDONED AREA: July 24, 1968

Shaded area indicates the scene of
the shoot-out the night before.

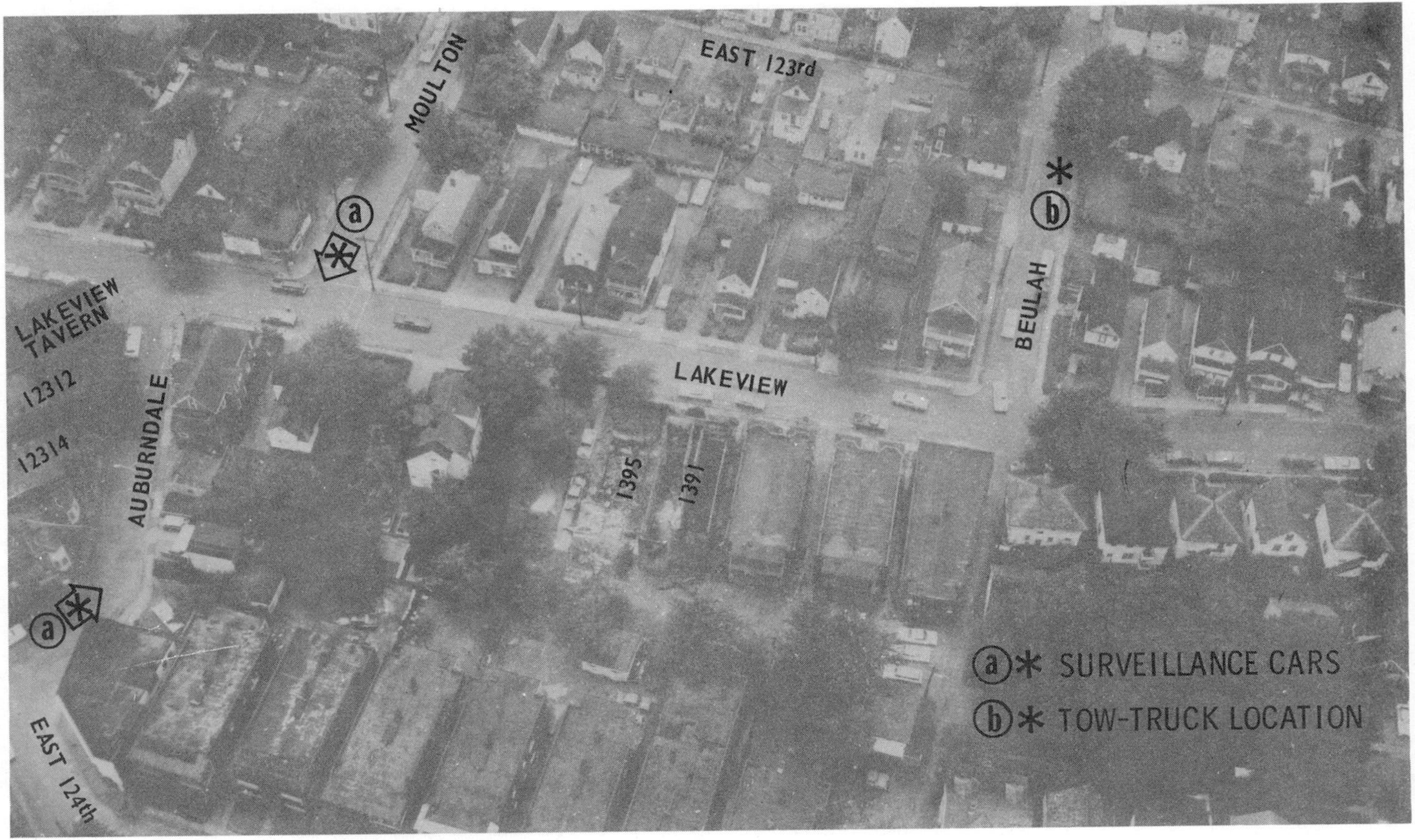

EAST 123rd

MOULTON

BEULAH

LAKEVIEW

1391

1395

AUBURNDALE

LAKEVIEW TAVERN

12312

1231A

EAST 124th

ⓐ ✳ SURVEILLANCE CARS

ⓑ ✳ TOW-TRUCK LOCATION

Fred "Ahmed" Evans in his Afro Culture Shop in April 1967.

In July 1966 riots in the Hough section resulted in a week of mass civil disorder—looting, sniping, vandalism, and burning.

In 1966 United Freedom Movement demonstrators attempted to block construction of schools in the Glenville area by throwing themselves into the pits and blocking equipment. The Reverend Bruce Klunder, the white minister who had helped organize the local chapter of CORE, place himself behind a bulldozer and was run over and killed.

The red brick apartment house at 12312 Auburndale, where Ahmed and other black nationalists lived, served as a nest for snipers in the Glenville battle.

The abandoned Cadillac parked on Beulah Avenue.

A policeman fires tear gas to flush snipers from the second story of the Lakeview Tavern.

Policemen crouch behind their cars while looking for snipers.   UPI Photo

Police seek the safety of their vehicles on Lakeview, north of Euclid Avenue.

The Cleveland Press-Bill Nehez

Police Officer Lt. Leroy Jones lies mortally wounded from sniper fire. The officer at right was later wounded.   UPI Photo

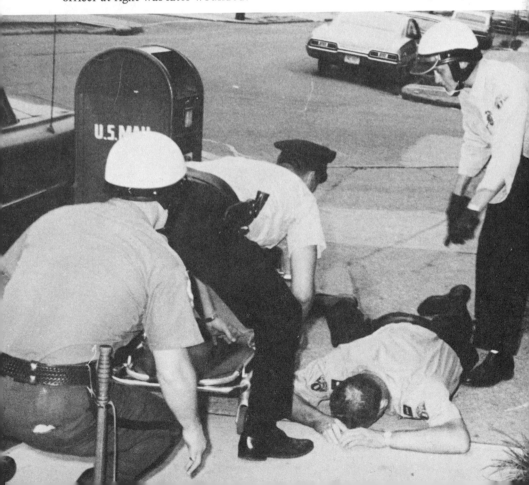

A police sharpshooter, armed with rifle with telescopic sight, aims his weapon.

UPI Photo

The bodies of two snipers lie in alley behind houses on Lakeview.

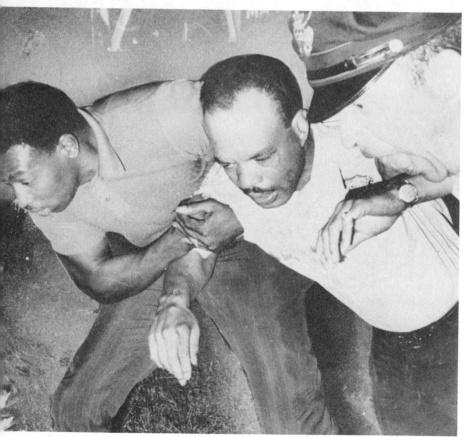

Patrolman Ernest Rowell suffered bullet wounds and was overcome by tear gas.

The man at left tied belts of ammunition around his chest.

Hospital attendants carry a policeman shot in the stomach.

National Guardsmen arrive at the scene.   *The Cleveland Press*-Bernie Noble

Police frisk suspects at the corner of Euclid and 105th Street. Fire-bombing and looting of stores continued throughout the night of July 23rd.

Herbert Reed a bystander
beaten by a gang, is led to a
hospital.

UPI Photo

A gutted police cruiser stands destroyed before a sign forecasting better days
ahead for residents of the predominantly Negro East Side. UPI Photo

The home of Rev. Henry Perryman at 1395 Lakeview engulfed in flames.

In the smoldering aftermath of five days of violence, 63 business establishments were damaged or destroyed. Property damage exceeded one million dollars.

The next morning Rev. Perryman views rubble. *The Cleveland Press*-Tony Tomsic

Ohio National Guardsmen stand by while smoke billows from the Linder Hotel.

The scene of violence on Superior Avenue at Lakeview—burning building and police cars.

Baxter Hill (with his hand to face) and members of PRIDE Inc. walk into sniper area.

On July 24, the following day, the Mayor's Committee marshals the black community.

Youths from PRIDE Inc. clean up debris after the night of violence.   Associated Press

Police search for looters.
The Cleveland Press-Bill Nehez

Loot from a furniture store is loaded carefully onto a car in broad daylight. UPI Photo

Guardsman holds looter at gunpoint in shop at 105th and Superior.

Mayor Carl Stokes walks the streets to survey damage.

Police prepare to raid the Esquire Hotel at 10602 Superior Avenue on July 26.

Three unarmed teenagers are brought out under police guard.

Mayor Stokes speaks with Harllel Jones, one of Cleveland's leading black nationalists and a member of the Mayor's Committee who was arrested two nights later for curfew violation and possession of weapons.

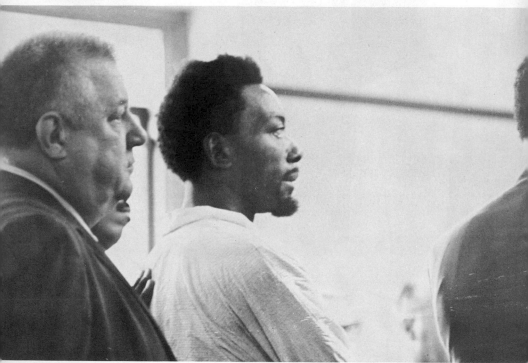

On July 26 Fred "Ahmed" Evans enters pleas of innocence to charges of shooting with intent to kill a police tow-truck operator, possession of narcotics, and possession of an automatic rifle.

Fred "Ahmed" Evans sits in the jailhouse.

Black nationalists demonstrate outside the courthouse during Ahmed's trial.

Fred "Ahmed" Evans, his wrists and ankles shackled, arrives at Ohio State
Penitentiary in Columbus after he was sentenced.

Chapter 1

PRELUDE TO THE SHOOTING

In the early years of the Republic, Cleveland was a small inland port settled by New Englanders who had moved westward, with a smattering of German merchants and Irish workers along the docks on the south shore of Lake Erie. Far into the 19th century, Cleveland kept the complexion of a New England town. In the years following the Civil War, however, surging commercial growth and industrialization brought to Cleveland an influx of immigrants from eastern and southern Europe. By 1910 these immigrants and their children made up 75 percent of the central city's population. Separated from the old inhabitants by language, customs, and religion, finding the doors to power and social acceptance closed to them, the immigrants retreated to ethnic enclaves of their own. Gradually they gained power in the city's politics, but the enclaves and ethnic loyalties remained. Later in the 20th century, especially after World War II, growing Cleveland experienced an influx of Negroes out of the South and Appalachia. In time, blacks constituted a sizable but powerless and excluded minority in Cleveland.

The recent history of the Negro struggle for equality in Cleveland parallels that of other American cities. In the early 1960's, when the civil-rights movement was gaining force in America, several small groups were formed in Cleveland. As elsewhere, white participation was welcomed, and a white minister and his wife were among the prime organizers of the Cleveland chapter of the Congress of Racial Equality (CORE) in 1962. By 1963 there were some 50 separate civil-rights groups in Cleveland, ranging from the moderate National Association for the Advancement of Colored People (NAACP) to CORE (then considered radical) to the Black Muslims (then, and now, even more radical).

In the spring of 1963, the Cleveland NAACP made a move toward establishing unity among the various groups. Its efforts to unite with the more militant groups may have been less an expression of a new militant spirit than of the political instinct to keep alive and enhance its own standing in the community. The effort succeeded; out of a series of meetings during the hot nights of June emerged a new coalition, calling itself the United Freedom Movement (UFM). Its integrated membership included inner-city ministers, leaders of the Jewish community, traditional Negro leaders, and some of Cleveland's new breed of angry young black men.

At best, the new alliance was tenuous. Much of its success would depend on how well it could assure cooperation and unity from so many diverse factions. A balance would have to be struck between moderate and militant approaches. And to survive, the UFM would have to demonstrate that it could produce results.

The UFM's first confrontation, over the hiring practices of contractors building the city's Convention Center, ended in no victory. In the fall of 1963, the alliance turned its attention to the city's school system. Although many Negro children were bussed to alter the segregated system, there was evidence that receiving schools contrived to separate these children from the white students. Relatively few of Cleveland's schoolchildren were in integrated classrooms. The UFM set a list of demands before the Board of Education, with a deadline of September 23 for compliance. The Board and UFM representatives met in a series of closed meetings, and on deadline day basic agreement seemed to have been reached. UFM spokesmen, however, argued that informal agreements in closed session were not official and binding. The following evening, after hearing a report from the steering committee, UFM members voted to picket the Board of Education.

The Board of Education responded to the picketing by scheduling a public meeting September 30, at which it promised to take steps toward "fullest possible integration consistent with sound educational practice" in the receiving schools. The board also promised to create a Citizens' Council on Human Relations to encourage true integration. For the moment, the UFM was triumphant.

By January 1964, UFM leaders concluded the board was not living up to its promises. Meetings with the board only deepened the frustration. To escalate the pressure, the UFM decided to take its picket lines to schools where black children were being bussed. The first two demonstrations, on January 29, brought forth angry mobs of whites. At one of the target schools, demonstrators were forced off the sidewalk as a mob tried to push them in the path of passing automobiles. The next day, a demonstration planned at Murray Hill School, in the heart of Cleveland's "Little Italy," produced a more serious confrontation. At 9:30 a.m., when the demonstration was scheduled to begin, a crowd of angry whites had already surrounded the school. Many were young, and many had been seen at the demonstrations the day before. Reports that the mob had formed deterred the demonstrators from attempting to march on the school. Sensing that the demonstrators would not march, the crowd moved to a busy intersection in Little Italy and began to attack Negroes driving by in their automobiles.

Throughout the day, the mob remained and continued to attack those perceived as "enemies"—enemies that included a number of newsmen. At about midday, the mob attempted to charge the area where the demonstrators had assembled. While police lines checked the advance of the crowd, the demonstrators left to assemble at another location several miles away. By late afternoon, any thought of a march on Murray Hill School was out of the question.

The Murray Hill incident was the UFM's fiery baptism and a clear signal of the deepening rift between Cleveland's blacks and whites. It was also a demonstration of the powerlessness of the Negro community, as evidenced by the official response from City Hall. Mayor Ralph Locher took the position that the school question was outside his jurisdiction. And while the violence lasted, he considered requesting an injunction against the picketing. The police were also a bitter disappointment to the civil-rights leaders. There had been no arrests despite the fact that for an entire day the Murray Hill mob roamed the streets beating Negroes, newsmen, anyone who enraged them, and throwing rocks and bottles at passing automobiles.

The rift grew even deeper when, on February 3, 1964, demonstrators staged a sit-in at the Board of Education building. Police forcibly removed them the next day. The UFM had already lost the sympathy of City Hall and the Board of Education; now the news media became disenchanted. The protest had gone "too far," it had become too "radical," the limit of tolerance had been reached. The community reaction also opened wounds within the UFM itself; while the more militant members were demanding further and more extreme measures, the NAACP faction openly worried about the consequences of the heightened level of protest.

On February 4, the UFM won a temporary victory. The Board of Education agreed to immediate diffusion of the bussed students on a level designed to induce integration. In March, however, it was evident that the board was pushing forward the construction of three schools in the Glenville area, the black neighborhood that was to be the scene of racial violence in 1968. These schools would, by their location, introduce segregation into the school system once more.

UFM demonstrators, on April 6, joined the Hazeldell Parents Association, a group of Glenville residents, in picketing one of the school construction sites. A new tactic was introduced: demonstrators threw themselves into construction pits and in the way of construction equipment. The next day the demonstration was carried to another construction site. The tactics remained the same. The only difference was the result: the Reverend Bruce Klunder, the white minister who had helped to organize the local chapter of CORE, placed himself behind a bulldozer and in the confusion was run over and killed.

Police sought to end the confrontation by dragging demonstrators away. As word of Klunder's death spread, however, further violence became inevitable. Bands of angry Negroes roamed the streets, looted stores, and battled police late into the night. Klunder's death would be long remembered in Cleveland's black community.

Blocked by a court injunction against further interference with school construction, the UFM—over the objections of its conservative members—turned to a new tactic: a boycott of the schools. On Monday, April 20, about 85 percent of the Negro students in Cleveland's public schools stayed home. The boycott was a Pyrrhic victory. Nonattendance of blacks at predominantly white schools was precisely what many white parents wanted. The boycott had not been important in terms of money, power, or lasting prestige—the important "values" of the power structure.

In succeeding months, a new superintendent of schools, Dr. Paul Briggs, significantly reduced the crisis. Briggs shifted emphasis from integration to quality education in each neighborhood. The shift undercut the efforts of the UFM. The emphasis on quality education in their own neighborhoods gained increasing acceptance in the Negro community, especially as the concept of "Black Power," with its emphasis on racial separatism, found more and more adherents.

*   *   *

"Black Power" gained in popularity in the black community during 1965, but it sent shivers of anxiety into the white enclaves of Cleveland. That summer, Clevelanders witnessed on their television sets racial disturbances in other cities, including the riot in Watts. In the fall of 1965, several organizations of black militants emerged in Cleveland, led by black nationalists. Traditional organizations such as the NAACP, and now even CORE, had increasing diffi- culty generating support from the white community. The only organization that continued to provide moral and financial support to the black groups was the Council of Churches, and its resources were limited.

In view of the mounting tensions between the white and black communi- ties, outbreaks of violence were not wholly surprising. Beginning early in 1966, gang fights and physical assaults plagued the Superior-Sowinski area. The Sowinski area, like the Murray Hill area, has been a white ethnic enclave in Cleveland's troubled East Side. As with the Murray Hill area, antagonism toward Negroes runs high in Sowinski. The Superior area bordering Sowinski is predominantly Negro.

The attacks and gang fights continued throughout the spring. Negro youths were responsible for some of the assaults, white youths for others, but to the Negro community it was apparent that police responded much more quickly and effectively when the victims were white. "If you're going to beat up those niggers," a policeman is said to have told a white gang, "take them down in the park [Sowinski Park] where we can't see it." On Wednesday evening, June 22, two Negro youths were attacked by a gang of whites. A crowd that gathered at Superior Avenue and 90th Street confronted police with their complaints, describing the attackers and pointing to the car they had ridden in, but the police made no move to investigate. Some in the angry crowd threw rocks and bottles. Negro leaders met with the police the next day; the police responded to their grievances by saying they had problems all over the city, that they were understaffed and overworked, that not every in- cident could be investigated, that incidents like Wednesday evening's attack occur all the time in racially mixed neighborhoods.

Violence broke out again Thursday evening. A Negro youth was shot, ac- cording to eyewitnesses, by two white men in a blue Corvair. The description seemed to implicate the owner of a supermarket on Superior Avenue. Since the police would not take any action, Negro youths took the initiative: the supermarket was burned to the ground. Other white-owned businesses were harassed during the evening's disturbance.

After still another night of violence, Mayor Locher met with Negro resi- dents of the troubled area on Saturday, June 25. He promised to investigate their grievances. The tension subsided, at least for the moment.

*   *   *

Superior Avenue, scene of the June 1966 disturbances, is a broad thorough- fare that carries Cleveland officeworkers home to the comfortable suburbs of East Cleveland and Cleveland Heights. South of Superior Avenue, roughly embracing the numbered streets between the seventies and the nineties, is the neighborhood of Hough (pronounced "huff"). It is a residential area of dete- riorating framehouses, old apartment buildings, dwellings vacant and vandal- ized, occasional small shops, and neighborhood bars. Since the mid-1950's, Hough has been a predominantly Negro slum.

On the evening of July 18, 1966, a sign appeared on the door of a bar at 79th and Hough Ave.: "No Water for Niggers." Residents of the area were enraged. A crowd gathered. The manager of the bar and another white man paraded in front of the bar armed with a pistol and a shotgun. Police arrived and, in their attempt to "disperse the crowd," began to push and shove individuals from the vicinity of the bar. Nearby stores became the targets of rocks. The crowd began to spread; the Hough riot had begun.

For one full week Cleveland was immersed in mass civil disorder. In many ways the violence resembled the earlier violence of Watts: looting, vandalism, burning, sniping. Initially, it was contained in a small area: between 71st Street on the west and 93d Street on the east, and including half-a-dozen blocks north and south of Hough Avenue. On July 20, the third night of violence, sporadic damage was reported in a much wider area, including parts of Kinsman on the south and Glenville on the east. It included thrown fire bombs, some looting, and attempts to divert the police with false fire alarms.

The damage in Hough was extensive. Before rainfall hit Cleveland on Sunday night, July 24, and the violence subsided, four persons (all Negro) had been killed, countless others injured, and whole blocks of buildings had been nearly totally leveled. More than 2,200 National Guardsmen had been called in to patrol the streets. And if Cleveland's racial relations were becoming polarized before the Hough riot, there was no doubt that the split was profound after it was over.

The grand jury of Cuyahoga County, in special session, began its investigation of the disturbances on July 26. In its report, issued August 9, the jury blamed the disorders on—

> a relatively small group of trained and disciplined professionals at this business . . . aided and abetted, wittingly or otherwise, by misguided people of all ages and colors, many of whom are avowed believers in violence and extremism, and some of whom also are either members of or officers in the Communist Party.

The conspiracy theory and the suggestion of Communist domination readily found adherents, and Mayor Locher congratulated the grand jury for having "the guts to fix the approximate cause which had been hinted at for a long time, that subversive and Communist elements in our community were behind the rioting."

Few in the black community were persuaded by the grand jury report. They could not fail to note that no Hough residents sat on the panel, and that the foreman of the grand jury, Louis B. Seltzer, editor of the *Cleveland Press*, was being sued at the time of the investigation by a black nationalist leader for calling his organization a "gun club." Suspicions of bias were fed by the report's references to the black leader, Lewis Robinson, as one dedicated to "inciting these youths to focus their hatreds" and to "indoctrinating them with his own vigorous philosophy of violence."

On August 22, a biracial review panel, composed wholly of citizens associated with the Hough area, began its own investigation. Their report concluded that "the underlying causes of the rioting are to be found in the social conditions that exist in the ghetto areas of Cleveland."

"To many," they noted, "it seemed almost inevitable that such neglect and disregard would lead to frustration and desperation that would finally burst forth in a destructive way." As to the influence of Communist agitators: "We would believe that an individual living in such poverty as exists in Hough needs no one to tell him just how deplorable his living conditions are."

A week later, controversy over the causes of the rioting reached into the hearing rooms of Washington. Testifying before Senator Ribicoff's committee investigating urban problems, Mayor Locher was confronted with the U.S. Attorney General's conclusion that "it would be a tragic mistake to try to say that the riots are the result of some masterminded plot." Mayor Locher, however, persisted. Locher argued: "I would disagree with the statements of the Attorney General, and I would wholeheartedly agree with the conclusions made by the grand jury report."

*   *   *

There matters stood at the end of the long hot summer, a war of conflicting viewpoints hardened to a standstill as autumn arrived and quietly passed into winter. Then it was 1967, and perceptive observers looked ahead to another summer of racial violence in Cleveland. As early as April 6, a *Cleveland Plain Dealer* reporter noted: "Even very rational, very hopeful men and women believe that Cleveland will be on fire this summer."

Like a seismograph picking up faint tremors that warn of a major earthquake, the April newspapers recorded a number of fires on Cleveland's East Side that may have been set by arsonists, and a series of lootings around 105th Street, eastward of the scene of the Hough riot. The Cleveland Subcommittee of the Ohio State Advisory Committee to the U.S. Commission on Civil Rights visited the Hough area and saw there ample evidence of the poverty and frustration that would breed another riot.

> Store fronts are boarded up. Unoccupied houses have been vandalized. Stench rises from the debris-filled basements of burned-out buildings. Litter fills street curbings. Garbage and trash are scattered in yards and vacant lots. Recent surveys indicate that in some census tracts as much as 80 percent of the 16-21 age group is unemployed or school dropouts and that 25 percent of the midyear high school graduates seeking work are unable to find jobs.

The subcommittee's report noted that women in Hough were paying high prices for low-quality food in neighborhood grocery stores, using welfare checks that were inadequate for a decent standard of living. The State government, the report charged, has been indifferent to the plight of Hough residents; so have the local authorities.

> The policeman, if you can find one, still shows little interest in vacant houses being stripped of equipment during daylight hours, or the prostitutes on parade, or the accosting of resident mothers and daughters walking home.

The national media shared the prediction that Cleveland was ripe for burning. In late June, Roldo Bartimole, a *Wall Street Journal* reporter, and Murray Gruber, a faculty member of Western Reserve University, published an article in the *Nation* entitled "Cleveland: Recipe for Violence." Their conclusion: "All the elements for tragedy are now present in this city, self-proclaimed 'Best Location in the Nation.' It may be too late for Cleveland, but there are lessons here for other cities that want to avoid disaster." A month later, in the *Saturday Evening Post*, staff writer John Skow noted: "It is hard to find a city resident who believes Cleveland will go unburned through the summer."

And yet, it didn't happen. While Tampa, Cincinnati, Atlanta, Newark, and Detroit experienced major disorders during the summer of 1967, the lid stayed on in Cleveland. Even Martin Luther King's peaceful efforts to press for better jobs for Negroes met with indifferences in the Negro neighborhoods of Cleveland that summer. Scorned by the mayor as "an extremist" when he arrived in April, King announced in May that Cleveland would be a "target city" for the Southern Christian Leadership Conference. His most severe tactic against employers discriminating against Negroes would be a boycott of their goods. King's campaign accomplished few of his aims, yet no one turned to violent means to abet his cause.

*   *   *

Explanations for Cleveland's quiet summer of 1967 abound. One contributing cause, perhaps of minor importance, was the channeling of hopes and grievances through the electoral process. Carl B. Stokes, a Negro candidate who in 1965 had come within 2,100 votes of becoming the mayor of Cleveland, was again challenging the incumbent, Ralph Locher. Having come so close, Stokes in 1967 had the avid backing and earnest hopes of Cleveland's black community.

In 1965 Stokes had run as an independent and gained an advantage from the multiplicity of candidates. This time he was forced into the Democratic primary race. Seth Taft, grandson of President Taft and a prominent Cleveland Republican, had threatened to withdraw as his party's candidate if Stokes ran as an independent, for Taft calculated that he would be a certain loser in a three-way race. Stokes, on the other hand, calculated that since he would have to run against Locher in either case, it would be easier to defeat him in the primary, when a lower turnout of voters could be expected.

Stokes was correct. In the primary election of October 4, he defeated Locher by a plurality of 18,000 votes. The decisive factor was the size of the Negro turnout. Although Negroes constituted only about 40 percent of the registered voters, 73.4 percent of them voted in the primary. Only 58.4 percent of the white voters cast ballots in the primary.

The campaign between Stokes and Taft was well fought. Both hired professional help for campaign promotion and poll taking; both made personal appearances and speeches frequently and throughout the city. They met in a series of televised debates in traditional Lincoln-Douglas style.

In the end, Stokes won, becoming the first Negro mayor of a major American city. His victory was initially interpreted as Cleveland's triumph over racial bigotry, an indication of a new openmindedness in American race relations. Examination of the voting data reveals this interpretation as optimistic. Support for Stokes was concentrated in the Negro wards, where he received 95 percent of the vote. In the predominantly white wards he received only 19.3 percent of the vote, and his support was lowest in the three wards with the highest concentration of white ethnic groups in the city.

As a Negro mayor, Stokes was the subject of critical scrutiny by the public and of high expectations from those who had felt ignored by previous, "machine" administrations. His first few months in office were wrecked with difficulties; there were minor political scandals involving some of his early appointees, and public squabblings among others of his administration. The turning point for Stokes came in the wake of Martin Luther King's assassination on April 4, 1968. While other cities erupted in violence, Stokes took to the streets to keep his brothers "cool," effectively invoking the help of black nationalists in keeping the peace. Cleveland stayed quiet, and white citizens of Cleveland were satisfied that in Mayor Stokes they had an effective guarantee against further racial disorders.

Many Clevelanders realized that there would have to be substantive changes in the Negro ghettoes, and they stepped forward in May to support the mayor's new program, "Cleveland: Now!," a campaign to raise $11,250,000 to finance programs ranging from youth employment to rehabilitation of housing to downtown economic development. Some of the projects were eligible for Federal matching funds, and on July 2 Vice President Humphrey came to Cleveland to announce a $1.6 million grant to the Negro-run Hough Area Development Corporation for a program to help small businesses in the riot-torn neighborhood. By then, pledges to the "Cleveland: Now!" campaign from businesses and citizens had reached the $4 million mark.

With optimism, and with a sense of satisfaction over progress being made, Cleveland entered the summer of 1968. But some who could see beneath the calm surface were not optimistic.

*   *   *

On the night of the primary election in 1967, a black militant leader, cavorting in the street, jubilant over Carl Stokes' victory, raised his hand in a good-will gesture toward a squad car of police nearby and shouted "Peace!" For Fred Evans, who had taken the Afro name of "Ahmed," it was a rare moment of truce in his personal war with the police.

Early in 1967, Ahmed Evans had been arrested and convicted of assaulting police officer James Payne, a Negro. The war with the police was not, by Evans' assessment, one sided; three times during 1967 police had closed down his Afro Culture Shop and Bookstore, on Superior Avenue, for alleged "sanitary violations." In interviews Evans referred to the police, in classic black-nationalist fashion, as "the repressive element in a white establishment."

Born in Greenville, S.C., in 1931, Evans was one of 12 children. His father was an unskilled worker in a textile plant. In the late 1930's, seeking a better opportunity, the family moved to Cleveland. Evans enrolled in public school but quit before graduating from Rawlings Junior High. Tall and gangling, he recalls that schoolmates called him "Big Dumb." Convinced that he was really smarter than his peers, Evans decided to go to work. He held a variety of jobs before joining the Army in 1948.

During the Korean war, Evans served with a combat engineer outfit. He suffered back, shoulder, and head injuries when a bridge he was working on collapsed. When he was discharged in 1952, he was the recipient on half-a-dozen medals for meritorious service. Back in Cleveland, Evans drove a bus for the Cleveland Transit System, then, in February of 1954, reenlisted in the Army. This time his service was far less distinguished. Shortly after he was back in uniform, Evans was court-martialed for hitting an officer and sentenced to a dishonorable discharge and 2 years' confinement at the U.S. Army Disciplinary Barracks at Fort Crowder, Mo. Later his sentence was reduced to an undesirable discharge and he was released from Fort Crowder after a 7-month term.

Evans had claimed that the injuries he had incurred in Korea left him with severe headaches, partial loss of vision, and recurring paralysis of the right side. He also claimed to be subject to occasional blackouts. It was during one of these blackouts, he said during court-martial, that he struck the officer. The records of the Army physicians corroborate Evans' claims. Doctors found he was suffering from "psychomotor epilepsy." Further testing disclosed that he has a "paranoid-type personality." Army records state: "He has much hostility, normally under control, but under stress he exhibits aggressive behavior. This condition could become progressive, causing him to act psychotic-like under stress." After these examinations, the Army release was decided upon. Evans returned to Cleveland in October 1955, the next year he took a job with the Pennsylvania Railroad, and he worked for that company for the next 10 years.

In the early 1960's Evans became interested in astrology. "I say a flying saucer at 79th and Kinsman," he recalls of the experience that changed his life. "It hovered for awhile and disappeared. That started me thinking about the stars and God and I thought that here I was thirty-three and Jesus had died at thirty-three and I hadn't even got started yet. So I moved off by myself to study the science of astrology and philosophy."

In 1966, Evans was the disciple of an astrologer named Emmett (Toneli) Cobb. When Cobb was confined at Lima State Hospital for the Criminally Insane, Evans (now Ahmed) stepped in to fill the gap. Though dismissed as an eccentric even by some of the important young black leaders, Evans gained an increasing following in his neighborhood of Glenville. He wore Afro garb and he spoke the rhetoric of black nationalism. Like others of the new generation of militant leaders, most of whom had risen to power after the civil rights activities of the early 1960's, he had seen the inside of a jail, he preached black separatism and self-help in the black community, and he advocated violence in retribution to the hostility of the "sick" white society.

Ahmed Evans also indulged in prophecy. He made national news when, in March of 1967, he predicted that May 9 would be a "terrible day." A *Wall Street Journal* article featured his prediction:

> He [Ahmed] predicts May 9 will be the "terrible day" that the anger of this city's black ghetto erupts into violence—partly because, by his calculations, that will be the day when an eclipse of the sun darkens the sky.

May 9 passed without violence. While the rest of the world scoffed, Ahmed's misreading of the heavens seemed to cost him no loss of influence in Glenville. Young blacks continued to congregate in his Afro Culture Shop and Bookstore. In the summer of 1968 Ahmed's group received a grant of $10,300 from "Cleveland: Now!" funds to develop African crafts. From this benefaction, channeled through the Hough Area Development Corporation, it would have seemed that Ahmed Evans was at peace with the white establishment.

But the world that had scoffed at a false prophet had not heard the last of Ahmed.

Chapter 2

A MIDSUMMER'S NIGHTMARE

Glenville, lying near the northeast corner of Cleveland, is a neighborhood of two- and three-story houses with broad front porches and small front lawns. In the 1940's Glenville was a largely Jewish area; today it is very predominantly Negro. Except for pockets of deterioration, it stands in tidy contrast to the Hough area, lying to the west.

For Patrolman William Kehoe, performing traffic duty on the East Side, July 23, 1968, was a slow day. Shortly after noon he called headquarters for a possible assignment. Lt. Edward Anderson, traffic coordinator for the Cleveland Police Department, assigned him to check an abandoned automobile in the Glenville area. Anderson had received a telephone call about the car not long before. "It was just a routine call of an abandoned auto," he later recalled. "I told the gentleman we'd get to it as soon as possible. I couldn't promise action that day." Following standard procedure, Anderson did not ask the caller's name.

The car, a 1958 Cadillac, was on Beulah Avenue, between East 123d Street and Lakeview. The left front tire was flat; to Patrolman Kehoe, it appeared the car was a "junk car" that had not been driven for some time. Neighbors confirmed that the car had been there many days; none had any idea who owned it. At 1:25 p.m., Kehoe placed a parking ticket on the abandoned car, then filled out a routine report for the tow truck division of the police department.

Kehoe expected that the car would be towed away before the evening rush hour. But William McMillan and Roy Benslay, operating tow truck No. 58, had other assignments that kept them from the pickup in Glenville until dusk. They arrived on Beulah Avenue in their uniforms, which resemble standard police uniforms except that the jackets are of the Eisenhower type. Clevelanders commonly assume that the tow-truck operators are policemen, but in fact they are civilian employees and carry no weapons.

What happened next has been recounted by McMillan. After Benslay backed the truck up the Cadillac, McMillan emerged from the cab to check the license plate number against the assignment card. "The next thing I knew I was shot in the back. I turned around and saw a man with a shotgun firing from the side of a house on the corner of Lakeview."

McMillan ran to the front of the tow truck to take cover. A second shot hit him in the right side. "Another sniper was firing from the bushes just in front of the truck." Benslay, crouching in the cab of the truck, radioed for help. Then the shooting stopped.

43

"A Negro with a carbine in his hand walked up the sidewalk and stopped just across from me," McMillan told a reporter several days later.

"Are you one of the sons of bitches stealing cars?" the Negro asked him. McMillan pleaded that he was unarmed and rose from the street to show that he had no weapon. The Negro raised the carbine to his shoulder and took aim. McMillan ran toward 123d Street. As he turned the corner, another bullet hit him in the right side. McMillan kept running.

Halfway along the block a Negro woman shouted to McMillan and offered him refuge. Inside the house he telephoned the police department, but the lines were busy. When he heard sirens, McMillan left the house and walked northward on 123d Street. After turning right on Oakland Avenue he spotted a squad car, which rushed him to a hospital.

McMillan identified the Negro with the carbine as Fred (Ahmed) Evans.

He also offered an explanation of the event. "The snipers set up the ambush and used the tow truck as a decoy to bring the police in," he said. "They had their crossfire all planned. We all were sitting ducks."

McMillan's ambush theory found ready acceptance. Many Clevelanders, and at least two national news magazines, accepted it unquestioningly. But other events of that grim Tuesday, and the accounts of other eyewitnesses, cast doubts upon the ambush theory.

*   *   *

Ahmed lived in an apartment in a two-story, red brick house at 12312 Auburndale, a block and a half from the scene of the tow-truck shooting. On the evening of July 23, shortly before the tow-truck incident, he had visitors: George Forbes, the city councilman from Ahmed's area, and Walter Beach, a former halfback for the Cleveland Browns, who was the director of the Mayor's Council on Youth Opportunities. According to a summary of events, issued later by the mayor's office, the meeting lasted from 7:50 p.m. to 8:05 p.m.

Forbes and Beach had come from a meeting at City Hall where Ahmed had been the subject of anxious discussion. The meeting, which began at 2:30 that afternoon, had been called by Inspector Lewis Coffey of the Cleveland Police Department. Coffey had intelligence reports, which the police department had obtained chiefly through the Federal Bureau of Investigation, that warned of an outbreak of violence planned for Cleveland the next morning, July 24, at 8 a.m. The central figures in the outbreak would be Ahmed and his group, the Black Nationalists of New Libya.

Ahmed's group, according to the reports, had been assembling an arsenal of handguns and carbines and stashing them in Ahmed's apartment. Some of the group had gone to Pittsburgh, Detroit, and Akron on Sunday night to collect semiautomatic weapons; a further trip to Detroit was planned for Tuesday evening, July 23. In addition to the Wednesday morning outbreak, the reports added, there was the possibility of simultaneous outbreaks in other Northern cities.[1] In Cleveland, five Negroes would be the targets of assassination: Mayor Carl B. Stokes, Councilman Leo Jackson, William O. Walker (publisher of the Negro newspaper, *The Cleveland Call & Post*), Baxter Hill, and James Payne. Four of the targets were prominent Negroes; the fifth, James Payne, was the patrolman Ahmed had been found guilty of assaulting.

The truth of these reports was questionable. Police doubted that a trip to both Pittsburgh and Detroit had been made in one night. The reports came from a single individual, a member of Ahmed's group who apparently was not an infiltrator but a man accustomed to selling information to the FBI and the Cleveland police. Other intelligence sources did not corroborate his story. Those who had talked to the informer on the telephone suspected he was under the influence of drugs.

The reports were serious enough, however, to warrant considerable attention. On Tuesday morning, Cleveland police checked various aspects of the intelligence reports. They learned that on Monday, black nationalists had been in Higbee's, a downtown department store, examining high-powered deer rifles with telescopic scopes. Nationalists had been seen buying bandoliers (links of ammunition for automatic weapons), canteens, and first-aid kits from a downtown army surplus store. There was some uncertainty whether the nationalists included Ahmed or any of his group.[2]

Mayor Stokes was in Washington, D.C., that day, participating in a discussion entitled "Is the Big City Dying?" In his absence, Clarence James, the law director (a position similar to city attorney or solicitor) participated in the City Hall meeting as "acting mayor." While the meeting was in progress, Mayor Stokes placed a routine call from Washington to his office. Informed of the potential trouble, he told James to telephone Baxter Hill, the director of Pride, Inc., a community self-help organization, and a member of the Community Relations Board. Unable to reach Hill, James summoned to the meeting Councilman George Forbes, who was also familiar with Ahmed and his group.

Discussion turned from the intelligence reports to tactics for coping with the developing situation. There were no grounds for arresting Ahmed and too little to establish "probable cause" for obtaining a search warrant. By the laws of Cleveland and Ohio, mere possession of handguns or rifles is not illegal. While possession of automatic and semiautomatic weapons *is* illegal, there was only the informer's report to indicate that Ahmed and his group possessed such weapons. Even if there had been something in the informer's story to establish probable cause, he could not be used to testify without "blowing" his cover.

According to the informer's story, Ahmed and his group were planning a trip to Detroit Tuesday evening to obtain illegal automatic weapons. That being the case, Inspector Coffey advised, the police should establish a surveillance near Ahmed's house. Furthermore, it ought to be a moving surveillance, not a stationary one—roving police cars rather than parked ones. Ahmed's neighborhood was residential, his and nearby streets were narrow, and a parked car full of men—especially if they were white police officers—would attract notice. Moreover, Ahmed often stationed guards at his home to watch for police, sometimes sending them on "patrols" to hunt for police on nearby streets. Enough cars were available for an effective moving surveillance, and the police department would assign to the task as many Negro officers as it could.

One other aspect of the informer's story demanded attention. Although police investigation had failed to find confirming evidence of an assassination plot, a decision was made to provide a security guard for the five Negroes mentioned as potential victims.

Councilman Forbes and Walter Beach agreed to talk to Ahmed, to try to cool him down and work out a solution to his known grievances. Forbes and Beach knew, as many others knew, that Ahmed was angered over apparent discriminations against him in recent weeks. With the grant he had received from "Cleveland: Now!" funds, Ahmed was in the process of refurbishing a dilapidated and long-vacant store on Hough Avenue, converting it into an Afro-American culture shop. After investing considerable effort on the cleanup, he was notified by the white landlord that he could not use the store. And now he was being evicted from his apartment on Auburndale. After legal proceedings, a 24-hour notice was served by bailiffs earlier on Tuesday. (The apartment actually was not his; it was rented by a 16-year-old who had taken the African name of Osu Bey.)[3]

After the City Hall meeting broke up about 6 p.m., Forbes and Beach drove toward the East Side. On the way to Ahmed's home they stopped on Superior Avenue at the Afro Set, a shop and gathering place for young militants. Harllel Jones, leader of the Afro Set, was not there, but Forbes and Beach talked to one of the young members of the group who agreed to accompany them to Ahmed's home. The three drove eastward on Superior Avenue, then turned south on Lakeview. At the corner of Moulton Avenue, which is close to the intersection of Lakeview and Auburndale, they saw an unmarked car "full of white people." It was glaringly evident that the police had established a stationary surveillance rather than a moving one. In fact, another surveillance car was facing Ahmed's apartment building from the opposite direction, parked where Auburndale joins East 124th Street. Both cars contained only white officers; both were in plain view of Ahmed's home.

Beach steered his car left onto Auburndale and parked in front of Ahmed's apartment building. As the three men emerged from the car, Ahmed called to them from a narrow passageway next to the building. In a backyard conference, he poured out his apprehension about the police surveillance. There were, he said, even police on the roof. The police had harassed him before; he was afraid the surveillance was leading up to another incident of harrassment. He urged Forbes and Beach to try to get the surveillance removed. The men also discussed Ahmed's eviction problems, and Forbes and Beach promised to do what they could.[4]

When the conference ended, the visitors felt they had satisfied Ahmed. As they were leaving, he told them to give a message to Mayor Stokes: "Tell the Big Brother downtown that everything is going to be all right."

Forbes decided that there was nothing he could do at the scene to have the surveillance removed. As a councilman, he knew the police who usually work in his district, but the surveillance teams were from a special unit. He judged they would not recognize him or listen to him.

The three men drove westward on Superior Avenue, stopping first at the Afro Set, then at a grocery store whose owner was a close friend of Ahmed's. The grocer was not there. Forbes and Beach, having left the third man at the Afro Set, then tried unsuccessfully to find Harllel Jones at his home on Hough Avenue. At a nearby office of the Cleveland Legal Aid Program, Forbes telephoned Joseph F. McManamon, Cleveland's safety director, to ask that the surveillance be removed. McManamon advised him to call Mayor Stokes, who had returned from Washington, and gave him the mayor's private phone number. While Forbes and Stokes were on the phone discussing what they could do about Ahmed's problems, a voice broke in to say that there was an emergency call for the mayor. Stokes asked Forbes to call back in about 5 minutes.

Forbes and Beach returned to the home of Harllel Jones, this time finding him there. While they were talking, a member of the Afro Set came in to report that shooting had begun in Glenville. Forbes called the mayor. Stokes already had the news. The emergency call had come from Safety Director McManamon. The Glenville disturbance had been ignited.

*   *   *

Who shot first? And at whom? Various accounts of where, how, and why the shooting started have appeared. Even after extensive investigation, questions remain unanswered.

Accounts of the activities of the surveillance teams, and of what they observed, have been provided by the policemen in the surveillance cars. Three patrolmen—O'Malley, Sweeney, and Gallagher—were in the unmarked car at 124th and Auburndale, facing westward toward Ahmed's house. When they arrived at 6 p.m., about a dozen Negroes, including women and children, were on the porch at 12312 Auburndale. About half were dressed in Afro garb, the others conventionally. The policemen kept watch through binoculars. Later in the evening, shortly before Councilman Forbes and Walter Beach arrived at the apartment, they saw Ahmed himself arrive in a red Volkswagen. Evidently no one was on the porch at this time.

Shortly after Beach and Forbes left, according to James O'Malley, a Negro carrying a carbine came out of 12312 Auburndale and stood guard. Ahmed came out a short while later, followed by about 16 others carrying arms and wearing bandoliers. The man who had come out first crossed the street, dropped to his knees, and pointed his rifle toward the surveillance car. O'Malley radioed for instructions and was told to get out of the area immediately. The time, he recalls, was 8:20 p.m.

Patroman Gallagher, driving the surveillance car, turned left onto 124th Street to escape from the area. As they were leaving, O'Malley saw two men get into a Ford station wagon and set off in pursuit of the surveillance car. The policemen heard a shot; it did not hit their car. Moments later the station wagon halted the pursuit, turned around, and headed back toward Auburndale.

Patrolmen Thomas Gerrity and Thomas Horgan were in the other surveillance car parked at the corner of Lakeview and Moulton, facing Ahmed's house from the opposite direction. They, too, observed the people on the porch, the later arrival of Ahmed in the red Volkswagen, and the arrival and departure of Councilman Forbes and Walter Beach. When Ahmed's group came out of the house, according to Horgan, several of the men headed toward their surveillance car. The surveillance car turned left onto Lakeview, heading northward toward Superior Avenue, to escape. A green Chevrolet followed them; Gerrity and Horgan heard several shots, but none hit their car. Horgan broadcast a warning to other police cars to stay out of the area. As their car headed west on Superior Avenue, Horgan heard a broadcast about the tow-truck operator being fired upon. Gerrity and Horgan turned southward, back toward the scene of trouble. When they arrived within view of the tow truck, says Horgan, they saw the tow-truck operator running with his hands up and an armed black nationalist chasing him. Then the surveillance

car was struck by fire coming from 123d and Beulah. Bullets hit the wind-
shield and the hood and demolished the grille. Gerrity and Horgan returned
the fire, shooting toward two snipers hiding behind the tow truck, until their
ammunition was exhausted. Then they sought escape northward on 123d
Street. By the time they were back on Superior, all four tires of their surveillance car were flat. When Gerrity returned to the police station, a colleague
recalled, the 28-year-old patrolman was "dry-vomiting and shaking so hard he
put his hand on the letter basket and the whole table shook."

According to Lt. Burt Miller, who had been assigned by the police department to reconstruct the history of the events of July 23, other police cars
were on the scene when Gerrity and Horgan approached the tow truck. "They
engaged, with other cars that were arriving, in a fire fight with males that were
carrying weapons," he told a City Hall press conference on August 9. Thus,
police cars had converged on the scene and the full-scale shootout had begun.
Three males, according to Lieutenant Miller, were firing at police from two
corners of Lakeview and Beulah; a fourth lay, wounded or dead, on the sidewalk at 123d and Beulah.

By the testimony of the surveillance teams, then, they were the first to be
fired upon, not the tow truck. Rightly or wrongly, Ahmed regarded the obvi-
ous presence of the surveillance cars over several hours' time as threatening.
The tow truck, it now appears, was not the deliberate target of a planned ambush but arrived at the wrong place at the wrong time. Inspector Lewis Coffey
took this view in an interview published in the *Plain Dealer* 3 days after the
event. According to Coffey, the tow truck arrived on Beulah Avenue "almost
simultaneously" with the initial shootings at the surveillance cars. "Then he
gets it."

The validity of the ambush theory can be examined in the light of other
information. For one thing, it has been established that the owner of the
abandoned car cannot be implicated in any plot to draw tow-truck operators
or police to the scene. Henry R. Leftwich, owner of the 1958 Cadillac, had
loaned the car to a friend while he was hospitalized for long-term treatment
of a back injury. His friend was returning the car on Sunday, July 6, when it
"broke down" on Beulah Avenue. He left it there; 2½ weeks later, Leftwich
still had done nothing about removing the car.

Of the sequence of events on Beulah Avenue during the evening of July 23,
there were several eyewitness reports. Not all of them accord with the claim
of William McMillan, the tow-truck operator, that he was shot very soon after
arriving at the abandoned car. Residents of the area have reported seeing the
tow-truck officers examining the automobile for a period of time before the
outbreak of shooting. A man and his wife drove by the tow truck as McMillan was getting out to examine the Cadillac. They drove to the intersection of
Lakeview, turned left and proceeded two blocks to Superior, turned left
again, and in that time heard no shots. Other witnesses claim that the tow-
truck operators were confronted by an individual who seemed to argue with
them. This individual walked away, only to reappear with the snipers some
time later. One resident interviewed claimed that the individual who confronted the tow-truck operators then walked away and made a telephone call.
Such a call could have been directed to Ahmed and also could have prompted
the movement from Ahmed's home or given it direction after the movement
had started.

The official police log lends weight to the evidence, supplied by the accounts of surveillance-car activity, that the movement away from Ahmed's house, and some of the actual shooting, occurred before McMillan was shot. The tow truck placed its call for help at 8:28 p.m. The first radio report of shooting came 4 minutes earlier in a conversation between the dispatchery and Car 604 (which was not one of the surveillance cars). Car 604 gave its position as 123d and Beulah. Since this is close to the location of the tow truck, it tends to support the conclusion that the tow truck was inadvertently trapped in the crossfire between police and snipers.

A puzzling claim was made in a chronology of events released by the mayor's office at the press conference on August 9. According to this chronology, at 8:15 p.m. the tow truck "gets [a] call" to pick up the abandoned Cadillac. This invites the inference that some citizen had telephoned the police department Tuesday evening with the intention of luring the tow truck into a trap. Except in response to dangerous accidents, it is not usual operating procedure for a tow truck to be instructed by headquarters to go immediately to tow a car. And it has been established that the automobile had been examined earlier on Tuesday and the tow-sheet report prepared then.

Against theories of an ambush or well-planned conspiracy stands the evidence that on Tuesday evening Ahmed was annoyed and apprehensive about the police surveillance. He expressed such sentiments to Walter Beach and George Forbes. He had memories of police violence in Akron. "So we armed ourselves. And what followed was chaos."

In an interview published in the *Cleveland Press*, August 2, Ahmed offered his version of his movements after leaving the house:

> I was heading for the Lakeview Tavern [at the corner of Auburndale and Lakeview] when I heard some shots coming from the end of the street. Then one of the brothers passed me running. Some policemen in a blue detective's car opened up with a machinegun and he was dead. So I ran into a yard and I began trading shots with a policeman behind a parked car. I couldn't hit him. I wasn't coming anywhere close to him. And then my carbine jammed.

According to Ahmed, he then hid in bushes and tried to fix the carbine, but without success.

In an interview for this study, Ahmed said that he had rounded the corner and was walking on Lakeview when he heard the first shot. When he went to investigate, he saw the tow-truck operator running along Beulah. Then, he said, he heard what sounded like a submachinegun blast; he later concluded that this was the fire that killed Amir Iber Katir, one of his followers. (The account by Lt. Miller and the observations of a radio reporter who arrived at the scene support the conclusion that the first person killed was a black nationalist. The corner's autopsy revealed four bullet wounds: the right chest, right thigh, left leg, and left thigh.[5]) Ahmed has concluded: "We were ambushed, not the police."

An eyewitness recalled that Ahmed came down the street very coolly. By the time he got to Beulah, the shooting had begun. Ahmed, said the witness, was carrying an automatic weapon, and when he reached the corner he started firing.

Ahmed himself, he came down later. On his side, and when he came
down with the automatic rifle or machinegun, whichever it be, his rifle
drowned all the other guns. . . . He came down peacefully. He came
down the left side of the street and when he turned the corner, that's
when all hell broke loose.

Ahmed has admitted that he did not have total control of the situation.
There were many nationalists involved and he was only one. "I had come to
be the leader. But the night of the 23d, there was no leader. After we got
our guns, it was every man for himself."

*   *   *

In the 1-hour period between 8:30 p.m. and 9:30 p.m. on Tuesday evening, at least 22 people were killed or injured in the raging gun battle between
police and snipers. The major shooting occurred along Lakeview Avenue between Beulah Avenue and Auburndale, a distance of less than 300 yards, and
ranged no more than a block each way on side streets.

The area is no place to hold a shoot-out. Lakeview itself is narrow. The
side streets are even narrower, and some of them jut at odd angles. Houses
are close together, sometimes separated by narrow passageways. There is little
room to maneuver.

When a radio call for assistance went out about 8:30 p.m., it was an "all
units" call; any available unit in the city could respond. Police throughout
the city left their regular patrols and rushed to the scene, anxious to help
their comrades in trouble. A radio newsman estimated there were 40 to 50
police officers when he arrived at 8:45 p.m. Later there were "several hundred officers," according to the *Cleveland Press*. Nearby streets accumulated
long lines of abandoned patrol cars as police parked their cars as close to the
shooting as possible, grabbed their weapons, and ran to lend assistance.[6]

The battle that ensued was a combination of confusion and panic. Police
enthusiastically rushed into the area without knowing precisely, or even generally, what they were rushing into. The response had largely been personal
initiative rather than planned reaction and an orderly show of controlled
force. Each officer grabbed his gun and did what he could. "Perhaps some
snipers were shot and killed," a policeman recalled of his experience. "I fired,
mostly at shadows." No one assumed command. There was no orderly way
to report to headquarters and no way for headquarters to issue directives.
Police had largely abandoned their radios when they left their cars.

After the initial shooting, the violence clustered around three locations:
East 123d and Beulah (location of the tow truck); two adjoining houses on
Lakeview (1391 and 1395); and, the Lakeview Tavern and 12312 Auburndale
(Ahmed's residence).

Among the first to respond to the call for assistance were Patrolmen Joseph
McManamon and Chester Szukalski in Car 591. They approached the area
from the south, driving up 123d Street. "I didn't see any people, any children
or anyone playing," Szukalski recalls. "All I could see was the yellow tow
truck parked on the northeast corner of 123d and Beulah."

As McManamon pulled in front of the tow truck, shots hit the patrol car
on the passenger side where Szukalski was sitting. Both men crawled out the
driver's side, but Szukalski was hit before he escaped.

> I got hit in the right forearm first, but I couldn't see where the shots were coming from. I just knew they were coming from my right and from a higher elevation. As I tried to crawl to safety, I was hit in the right thigh. It was the third shot that hit me that really wrecked me. That one hit my right calf, causing a compound fracture of my right leg, then hit my left calf. By then I could hardly crawl. The pain was awful. I crawled about thirty or forty feet to a building, waiting for help. We [Szukalski and McManamon] could see other policemen in the area, but they couldn't get to us because the gunfire was, so intense and constant. We waited about fifteen minutes for our buddies to get us out.

McManamon was slightly wounded by fragments from the bullet that broke Szukalski's leg.

As Amir Iber Katir lay dying on the sidewalk and more police cars converged on the scene, the snipers on Beulah Avenue retreated across Lakeview into the narrow alley that is an extension of Beulah. With police in pursuit they turned right into the alley parallel to Lakeview and began exchanging fire with police from between the houses. Some forced their way into the two-and-a-half-story frame house at 1395 Lakeview and occupied the second floor. Beatrice Flagg was watching television in her first-floor apartment when the shooting started.

> They started shooting and I was afraid to look out. I told my kids to get down on the ground and pray. I looked out and there was an army of police there. I could hear a lot of loud swearing upstairs. I begged the police to stop shooting but they wouldn't listen. I barred the door because I didn't want anybody to get in and then I just got back down on the ground.

Mrs. Flagg and her children escaped from the house after tear gas began to fill her living room. Mrs. Henry Perryman, on the second floor with her 9-month-old baby, also managed to escape.[7]

Police then occupied the first floor of the house next door (1391 Lakeview). In the area between the two buildings, Patrolman Louis E. Golonka was shot and killed. Police, firing at armed men in the alley from windows of 1391 Lakeview, killed Sidney Curtis Taylor (Malik Ali Bey) and wounded Lathan Donald (Londue). From nearby bushes a man rose and tried to fire at police. Picking up Patrolman Golonka's shotgun, a policeman fatally shot the man, who was Bernard Donald (Nondu Bey), brother of Lathan Donald. The bodies of the three black nationalists—two dead, one severely injured—lay in the alley amid carbines and bandoliers until after midnight.

Another gun battle was raging at the intersection of Auburndale and Lakeview. Patrolman Kenneth Gibbons and Willard Wolff, in Car 505, had responded to the call for assistance and reportedly were the first to arrive at the intersection. Another policeman was on the scene, however: an unidentified plainclothesman struggling with a "young punk" near Ahmed's house. As they left the car to assist, a high-powered bullet hit the motor and the car exploded. Gibbons was shot and seriously injured; Wolff was killed.

Sgts. Sam Levy and Bill Moran also were among the first to arrive at Auburndale and Lakeview. They heard shots coming from backyards. Levy describes their response:

> We dodged through the yards and crawled along to the back of the
> Lakeview Tavern, where I saw shells on the ground. I got to the north-
> east corner of Auburndale and Lakeview and I saw some empty ammu-
> nition clips in the driveway behind the bar. I started up the driveway
> and I must have gone about three steps when I was hit. . . . I dove into
> the gutter and tried to get behind a car parked near the intersection.
> They kept shooting and I was hit again. They shot at anybody who
> moved.

Levy took refuge under the parked car. He was stranded for nearly an hour
before help could reach him.

Lt. Elmer Joseph entered Auburndale from Lakeview about the same time
that Sergeant Levy was wounded. He was on the sidewalk when he was hit;
he managed to get himself to cover. Lieutenant Joseph was also stranded for
almost an hour. Henry Orange, a 50-year-old civilian, was wounded at about
the same time, allegedly while assisting police. Patrolman Richard Hart was
shot in the back, apparently by a sniper hiding in a dark doorway, then hit
several more times as he writhed in the middle of Lakeview.

Lt. Leroy James and Sergeant Gentile stopped at Sixth District headquarters to "pick up extra weapons" after they heard the call for assistance. They
entered the battleground area from East 124th Street, thus approaching Auburndale from the east. They parked and continued to Auburndale on foot.
As Lieutenant Jones turned the corner onto Auburndale, Sergeant Gentile,
behind him, heard heavy fire. Gentile hurried around the corner, only to see
Jones fall to the sidewalk in the middle of the block. Gentile attempted to
approach Jones, but the heavy fire kept him from reaching his wounded
partner.

Patrolmen Angelo Santa Maria and Steve Sopko also rushed to the scene.
By the time they got there, so many police cars were in the area that they had
to park two blocks away. While Sopko headed in another direction, Santa
Maria ran behind the houses on Auburndale. From there he could see a police
officer lying on the sidewalk. "I yelled to other police under cover across the
street, 'Who is it?' They yelled back, 'Lieutenant Jones.' "

Then, says Santa Maria, he talked to several Negro bystanders, asking for a
volunteer to drive a car alongside Lieutenant Jones so that Santa Maria could
drag him into it. Several offered help; Santa Maria chose a man whom police
later identified as James E. Chapman, a 22-year-old filing clerk who lived next
door to the Lakeview Tavern. Santa Maria got into Chapman's car.

> I told him to drive up parallel to Jones and throw himself on the floor
> and I would try to drag Jones in. But cars were parked bumper to
> bumper. We both got out and separated, trying to get around them.
> On the sidewalk a sergeant met me. We decided to throw a smoke bomb
> for cover.

Then, according to the *Cleveland Press*, "the sergeant opened up with his submachinegun to protect Santa Maria, who went into the smoke to get Jones."
(Cleveland police are not issued automatic weapons, and it is against regula-
tions to possess them.) Santa Maria describes the rescue:

> I grabbed his legs and started to drag him out when I was hit in the
> back. I tried to crawl but I didn't get very far. Some policeman [later

identified as Patrolman Steven Marencky] dragged me, then threw me over his shoulder and put me in a police car.

Santa Maria did not know the identity of the Negro who was helping him nor what happened to him next. From newspaper accounts and the coroner's report, it is apparent that James E. Chapman died from a massive head wound, fired from an automatic weapon from a direction to his right and above him. The identification of Chapman as Santa Maria's helper was first made by police in a *Cleveland Press* article 8 days after the event. Chapman was proclaimed a hero, and Bluecoats, Inc., an organization that helps widows of policemen, departed from standard policy to present a thousand-dollar check to Chapman's widow.[8]

Two patrolmen made an attempt to rescue Sergeant Levy and Lieutenant Joseph, who lay wounded on the street, pinned there by sniper fire. Thomas Smith ran to Lieutenant Joseph, dragged him across the street to safety, then ran to Sergeant Levy, who was lying under a car. He dragged Levy from under the car, started to pick him up, and was shot in the right shoulder. "I spun around and then I was struck by crossfire and fell to the ground." Patrolman Ernest Rowell had joined in the attempt to rescue Levy.

> Smith was hit. I was hit as I dropped to the ground near Levy. Smith was still exposed. I managed to pull him near us. I couldn't get him under the car. So I put my legs over his head. He was moaning that he couldn't move his legs. I loosened Levy's shirt and partially stopped the bleeding. We kept assuring each other help would reach us. . . .
> Finally—it must have been an hour later—a tear gas cannister was accidentally triggered by another policeman. But that cloud was a welcome sight, even though it was burning our eyes. As the cloud covered the car, I jumped up and ran towards Lakeview Road. The gunfire was rat-tat-tat-ing in spurts. It was now or never.

Two other patrolmen, William Traine and James Herron, took advantage of the tear gas and headed toward the car protecting Levy and Smith. With the help of other policemen they got them placed on stretchers and rolled to an ambulance about 20 feet away.

Patrolman Leonard Szalkiewicz was wounded on Lakeview, near the intersection of Auburndale, as he was pushing a patrol car blocking the street. "At first I wasn't sure whether I was shot or whether I was cut by flying glass." Another patrolman, Anthony Sherbinski, was wounded about 9:30 p.m. as he shot at snipers from the second floor of the Lakeview tavern. A civilian John Pegues, was shot in the leg about the same time.[9]

By 9:45 the shooting had died down, and police were able to move into 12312 and 12314 Auburndale to search for suspects. A reporter at the scene counted 17 men and women, presumably all the occupants of the two houses, brought out, loaded into patrol cars, and taken to district headquarters for questioning. Fred (Ahmed) Evans was not among them. No casualties were found in the two houses. Four rifles and a number of boxes of ammunition were recovered from the houses, another rifle from a car parked nearby.

The next morning, at 9:30 a.m., police arrested and charged three individuals for participating in the shooting: John Hardrick, 17; Leslie Jackson (Osu Bey), 16; and Alfred Thomas, 18. All were found at 12314 Auburndale, the

house next door to Ahmed's. John Phillips, the arresting officer, later testified in juvenile court that he found Hardrick hiding in the bedroom where
three more high-powered rifles were also found. According to Phillips, Hardrick said he had been given his rifle by Ahmed around 5:30 p.m. on the evening of July 23. Ahmed showed him how to use the rifle and told him to be
on the alert. Jackson, said Phillips, had been given his rifle by a sniper who
came down from the roof of the building after the shooting started. Both
youths, Phillips told the court, admitted to firing their rifles "four or five
times" during the evening.

No other individuals apprehended in the vicinity of Auburndale and Lakeview were charged by police for participating in the shooting.

*   *   *

On the evening of July 23d, Henry Perryman, minister of a store-front
church on Superior Avenue, was on his way to Akron, scene of recent racial
disturbances, to help "cool things down." His car radio brought news of the
shootings in his Cleveland neighborhood. Perryman turned around and sped
homeward. He arrived back in Glenville to discover that police were firing at
snipers in his own house at 1395 Lakeview.

Distraught, fearful for the safety of his family, Perryman attempted to enter the house, but a policeman held him back. "That man saved my life," says
Perryman. He found his wife and 9-month-old son in safety across the street.
Eleven-year-old Michael Perryman, who had left the house early in the evening, was nowhere to be found.

A fierce gun battle raged around 1395 Lakeview, lasting long after the
shooting had subsided at Auburndale and Lakeview. Police reported that the
snipers were firing wildly from every floor of the house. They called to a
sniper in the basement to surrender, but he answered them with obscenities.
At one point, according to the police, a man came out of the house and fired
a weapon randomly from the areaway between 1395 and 1391. He returned
to the house, and, when he appeared at a window, police shot and felled him.
The shooting from the first floor stopped, but continued from the second.

Around midnight, a group of police attempted to storm the house. They
got through one door; a locked second door barred them from access to the
second floor. They shot off the lock but then encountered a steel wedge behind the door. Furniture and bedding were leaning against the door on the
other side. They could not get to the sniper on the second floor. The body of
the sniper who had been shooting from the first floor, they reported, lay on
the kitchen floor dead.

"At this time," Lieutenant Miller reported at the City Hall press conference on August 9, "the house erupted in flames." The cause of the fire has
not been determined, but residents of the area are convinced that the police
set the fire themselves. Henry Perryman has made a plea to the city of Cleveland for compensation for the destruction of his home.

Perryman watched his home burn to the ground; the house next door
(1391 Lakeview) catch fire and burn also. Police reported hearing shouts of
"Omar, Omar" and "Ali" come from within 1395. Perryman's 11-year-old
son had still not been found. Fire department units made no attempt to approach the burning structures to extinguish the flames.

Among others watching the buildings consumed in flames were Councilman George Forbes, Law Director Clarence James, Walter Beach, and three other black leaders: Harllel Jones, Wilbur Grattan, and Albert "Breeze" Forest. Forbes, Beach, and Jones, together with Baxter Hill, had been active throughout the evening trying to restore peace, trying to talk to the snipers but unable to get near because of the shooting. James had been touring the troubled area as the Mayor's eyewitness and reporter.

When the two Lakeview houses began to burn, Harllel Jones wanted to make sure that everyone had been removed from them. He, Forbes, Grattan, and Forest approached the burning buildings. As Jones got to the alley behind the houses, he noticed that the bodies of the shot snipers were still lying there. One of the bodies was beginning to burn; Jones dragged it away. Lathan Donald, still alive, was also in danger of catching fire. With the help of the other men, Harllel Jones got Donald onto a stretcher; Grattan and Forest began to carry the wounded man from the alley. According to the reports of those attempting to assist Lathan Donald, unidentified police officers (who had removed their badges) attacked Grattan and Forest, beating them severely, saying "Leave that nigger here to die." Grattan and Forest retreated without the stretcher, but managed to tell two Negro policemen about the incident before leaving the area.

All the while Forest, Grattan, and Jones were investigating the dead and wounded behind the burning buildings, Clarence James, Assistant Safety Director Frank Moss, and others remained by their cars at Beulah and Lakeview. There they became near victims of the chaos. James described what happened:

> Now there were a lot of shells exploding; it looked like they were burning shells. As I turned toward the car there were people lined up on the porches and everything, and an awful lot of police officers were there. I turned back toward the car. I heard two shots. It probably was my imagination, but I thought I heard the "zing" of one, and I dropped right down to my knees by the car. Frank Moss was just diagonally [across from me]. I could see him. He spun [around] and started to draw his revolver. . . . Boy, everybody was almost in a freeze position, and I got a little scared. . . . I made up my mind I was going to get the hell out of there.

James does not know who fired the shots, but he does not dismiss the possibility that the one that came close to him was fired by a policeman.

About this time, Grattan and Forest emerged from the alley, Forest bleeding and in pain. Clarence James and Harllel Jones took Forest to Forest City Hospital. There, James placed a call to Mayor Stokes. Stokes spoke with Harllel Jones, who was outraged over police conduct during the incident, and managed to calm him down. Later, Lathan Donald was brought to the prison ward of Cleveland Metropolitan General Hospital by two Negro policemen who had taken him from the alley.

Henry Perryman and his wife kept a vigil on their burning house late into the night. Two cars in their driveway went up in flames.

Perryman was injured in a scuffle with a young militant who had shouted at him: "This is only the beginning." The next morning, as Perryman picked among the ashes, looking for redeemable possessions, his son Michael, having spent the night at the home of friends, returned.

On July 30, a week after the incident, a city power shovel plied back and forth amid the rubble of the two houses, looking for the bodies of the two snipers whom police had reported occupying 1395 and who were presumed burned in the fire. No bodies were found.

*   *   *

At 11:11 p.m., before the fire in the Perryman house started, a call went out over the police radio: "1384 Lakeview: front door open, man wants to give himself up, wants [to surrender to] Negro policemen." A similar message went out at 12:24 p.m. This time, three white policemen, Sgt. Ronald Heinz, Patrolmen David Hicks and John Cullen, approached 1384 Lakeview to apprehend the man who wished to surrender. Fred (Ahmed) Evans emerged from the house, shirtless, wearing slacks and sandals.

The house from which Ahmed came was across the street from the Perryman house. The only times that 1384 Lakeview appeared in official police chronologies and records were the two broadcasts offering Ahmed's surrender.[10]

When Ahmed emerged, he was reported to have asked: "How are my people?" Told that at least three had been killed, he replied: "They died for a worthy cause." Ahmed said he had 17 in his group.

When police asked Ahmed where his weapon was, he pointed to the bushes in front of the house. The police found a toga, a loaded carbine, five boxes of ammunition, and a first-aid kit. Ahmed explained: "If my carbine hadn't jammed I would have killed you three. I had you in my sights when my rifle jammed." Before taking him to central headquarters, one of the policemen asked Ahmed: "Why did you start all this?" He replied, "You police have bothered us too long."[11]

Though the battle between police and snipers waged past midnight, the casualties of that battle occurred within the first hour of the shooting.

A chronology of events, issued by the Mayor's office on August 9, lists the following casualties:

Around E. 123d St. and Beulah

William McMillan (tow-truck operator)	wounded at	8:25 p.m.
Ptl. Chester Szukalski	wounded	8:30
Ptl. Joseph McManamon	wounded	8:30
Leroy Mansfield Williams (suspect)	killed	9:26(?)

Around 1391 and 1395 Lakeview

Ptl. Louis Golonka	killed at	8:35 p.m.
Sidney Taylor Curtis (suspect)	killed	8:40
Bernard Donald (suspect)	killed	8:40
Lathan Donald (suspect)	wounded	8:45

Around the Lakeview Tavern, 12312, and 12314 Auburndale

a. at Lakeview and Auburndale:

Ptl. Willard Wolff	killed at	8:30 p.m.
Ptl. Kenneth Gibbons	wounded	8:30
Sgt. Samuel Levy	wounded	8:45
Henry Orange (civilian)	wounded	8:45

Lt. Elmer Joseph	wounded at	8:45 p.m.
Ptl. Richard Hart	wounded	8:45
Ptl. Leonard Szalkiewicz	wounded	8:55
Ptl. Ernest Rowell	wounded	9:30
Ptl. Thomas Smith	wounded	9:30

b. at the Lakeview Tavern:

| Ptl. Anthony Sherbinski | wounded | 9:30 |
| John Pegues (civilian) | wounded | 9:30 |

c. in the vicinity of 12312 and 12314 Auburndale:

Lt. Leroy Jones	killed	8:45
Ptl. Angelo Santa Maria	wounded	9:00
James E. Chapman (civilian)	killed	9:00

Thus, by 9:30 p.m., the official casualty list read: 3 police killed, 12 injured (counting McMillan, the tow-truck operator); 3 suspects killed, 1 wounded; 1 civilian killed, 2 injured. The count shows 7 lives lost and 15 individuals wounded: a total of 22 casualties.[12]

REFERENCES

1. At a press conference on July 24, Mayor Stokes named four cities that, according to the intelligence reports, were targeted for simultaneous violence: Cleveland, Chicago, Detroit, and Pittsburgh. Others recall that two other cities were named in the reports: Akron, Ohio, and New York City.

2. In April 1969, during the murder trial of Fred (Ahmed) Evans, the prosecution established that a gun-buying spree had taken place and that Ahmed was one of the purchasers.

3. Other sides of the eviction stories were investigated by the *Cleveland Plain Dealer* and published Aug. 2. A spokesman for the owner of the shop on Hough Avenue said that after making a verbal agreement through her attorney to rent the shop to Ahmed, the owner, an elderly widow, decided not to rent the store "because it would take more than $1,000 to install toilets and repair the furnace at a time when negotiations had started to sell the building." Notified of this, the spokesman said, Ahmed continued to occupy the building and repair it, despite repeated protests. According to the spokesman, the issue of race was not involved, since renters of adjoining stores, belonging to the same owner, included Negroes.

   Osu Bey was notified on June 15, when his rent was 6 weeks in arrears, that he would be evicted from his apartment. The case was brought to court on July 22, and the eviction notice was served the next day. The owner of 12312 Auburndale said Bey had been permitting "as many as eight to ten couples" to sleep in the apartment, in violation of housing ordinances.

4. Ahmed had recently visited Akron during a racial disturbance. There he had witnessed a police attack on the office of a black nationalist group. "They had tossed tear gas inside, then barricaded all the doors. They blocked the people inside for about 15 minutes and then, when they were half-suffocated, they went inside and started hitting them with their billy clubs. Women and kids, too." On August 2 he would tell a *Cleveland Press* reporter: "When the police drove up on the 23d, we thought at first it might be just normal surveillance, but then we remembered Akron."

5. At the press conference on August 9, Lt. Miller said of the dead sniper: "This male has never shown up. He was removed while the fight went on . . . [he] disappeared." Amir Iber Katir, however, was the adopted name of Leroy Mansfield Williams, who was on the official casualty list. A reporter saw the body of the first felled sniper being borne by a group of Negroes toward a car some time after 9:15 p.m.; this agrees with the corner's report that the body of Leroy Williams

arrived by car at Huron Road Hospital about 9:25 p.m. In its reference to the body's original location as an "alley at Lakeview Road and E. 123rd Street," the coroner's report is not helpful, since the two mentioned streets run parallel south of Superior.

6.   The abandoned police cars were vulnerable to one of the tactics of urban guerrilla warfare. At 12:46 a.m. (then Wednesday morning) the following alert was broadcast over the police radio: "All Cars—Check all abandoned police cars for bombs prior to moving them."

7.   Mrs. Perryman denies newspaper quotations attributed to her that would indicate snipers barged into her apartment while she was there. According to her husband, who was away at the time, the first activity of which Mrs. Perryman and Mrs. Flagg were aware was the shooting by police, without warning, of tear gas shells and bullets into the house.

The *Call & Post*, on July 27, gave this version of the sequence of events: "Police ordered the Perryman home evacuated . . . to protect the occupants and to get vantage points from which they could flush out the snipers. The snipers later entered the abandoned Perryman home and used it as a sniper's [sic] post."

8.   Some people, including several close relatives of Chapman, did not accept the heroic version of Chapman's death. A friend of Chapman's claimed he saw him alive as late as 10 p.m. The angle of fire and type of weapon do not rule out the possibility that Chapman was killed by policemen. Police were reported to be using automatic weapons. In a late stage of the battle, some policemen were high off the street, occupying the second floor of the Lakeview Tavern. The coroner's description of the wound was interpreted as an indication that Chapman was shot from a distance (and thus probably by a sniper) but Alan Moritz, a noted pathologist who examined pictures of the wound, concluded that distance could not be determined by the shape of the wound. A reporter for the Negro weekly, the *Cleveland Call & Post*, attempted to investigate the Chapman case the day before the hero story was released and found police would divulge no details. The coroner's report, dated July 24, carried a notation that Chapman was killed while assisting police, but the report was not released to the public for nearly a week, during which time a reporter was denied access to it. The *Call & Post* reporter has concluded: "Whether Chapman was killed by the police or the snipers will probably remain a mystery forever." It was to be no idle mystery, however, since Fred (Ahmed) Evans was indicted for the murder of Chapman. Testimony at the trial cast further doubt on the heroic version of Chapman's death when the eminent pathologist Cyril Wecht said the fatal bullet was fired from no more than six inches. No sniper, of course, could have gotten that close to Chapman in the company of police.

9.   The circumstances of Pegues's injury were never spelled out by the police or other official agencies. An eyewitness gave his account in the *Cleveland Call & Post*. Arthur Redan, a 34-year-old bricklayer's helper, was in the Lakeview Tavern when police ran in and told the 10 customers and employees to lie on the floor. Other police came in and shoved the 3 women and 7 men down into the basement, firing at the ceiling in the process, then shot tear gas into the basement. John Pegues, said Redan, was wounded by a policeman during this episode. When the 10 were finally released from the gas-filled basement at 10:15 p.m., according to Redan, the women were pushed about and indecently handled by police, the men were dragged and pistol whipped, and all 10 were thrown into a police wagon, taken to Fifth District headquarters, and locked in a single cell "with John Pegues stretched out bleeding on a bench." Redan said Pegues was refused medical treatment until 5 a.m. Wednesday.

In an interview for this study, Dick Peery, a *Call & Post* reporter, said he witnessed this violence before police ordered him away from the tavern, disregarding his press credentials. He saw the men from the tavern being prodded with rifle butts, one of the three women doubled up in [extreme pain, the other two emerging from the tavern in] ripped clothes. Peery also interviewed a man who said he was driving through the area when police dragged him from his car, beat him severely, and called him a nigger and a cop killer.

10.   Detectives who later investigated the attic of 1384 Lakeview, where Ahmed had been, found cigaret butts and bullets but no spent shells. According to Joseph Turpin, a workhouse guard who lives at 1384, Ahmed broke in the house about the time the tow-truck shooting took place. (Turpin, who had been watching the tow-truck incident, insists that Ahmed did no shooting.) Ahmed went to the attic and, at least three times during the evening, yelled to Turpin that he wanted to stop the battle by surrendering. Turpin says he called the police in Ahmed's behalf at least five times.

11.   These statements attributed to Ahmed and published in Cleveland newspapers are the substance of what police told reporters Ahmed said at the time. At the beginning of his murder trial in Mar. 1969, Ahmed's lawyers were denied a motion to have these statements suppressed.

12.   There is evidence that some individuals who received injuries, mostly minor, were not included on the official casualty list. It is probable that snipers escaped from the scene, and some of these may have been injured. Injured or dead snipers may have been borne to hiding places by friends. Two policemen said they saw a sniper fall from the roof of an Auburndale house; then four people dragged him to a panel truck and drove away. Randel T. Osburn, Cleveland director of the Southern Christian Leadership Conference, says he saw a number of men running near Lakeview and Beulah and heading toward Superior: "One guy was running into an alley and he had been shot and he was holding his shoulder, all bloody. Two other fellows were carrying a second guy that we never heard anything else about, so I guess they made a clean getaway."

Chapter 3

REACTION: THE CROWDS,
THE POLICE, AND CITY HALL

Take an army of policemen, especially white policemen, into the ghetto, add a crowd of onlookers, and you have created a situation ripe for mass violence.

Just north of the Glenville battlefield lay Superior Avenue, a broad thoroughfare that carries U.S. Routes 6 and 20. A crowd began to gather on Superior soon after the shooting started, barely within eyesight range of the shooting on Lakeview Road. The crowd became unruly, heaving rocks at passing cars and jeering at the police swarming into the area. When the body of a dead or dying sniper was carried toward the intersection, the smoldering hatreds of the crowd were aroused. "Look what they've done to one of our brothers!" some were heard to say.

By 9:30 p.m., the crowd had grown huge. Most in the crowd were young; by one estimate, the average age was 22 or 23. Their mood was clearly hostile. "The crowd was berserk," one eyewitness recalls, and the police were frightened; they ran from their cars "like scared jack rabbits." A police car on Superior was hit by a Molotov cocktail; there was a "whoosh" and it went up in flames. The crowd scattered when ammunition in the car began to explode. A panel truck came down Superior and turned wildly directly into the crowd. The white driver was grabbed, pulled from the truck, and beaten to bloodiness. The crowd turned the truck over and set it afire. Herbert Reed, a 21-year-old patrolman, was pulled from his car at East 124th and Superior by a gang of Negro youths and beaten savagely. Two news cars containing valuable equipment were set afire and destroyed.

As they had done on the first night of the Hough riot in 1966, the police sensed that the crowd was beyond control and they abandoned the situation. As the huge crowd began to move, it found itself free of police restraint. A few black policemen remained to prevent cars with white occupants from running the Superior Avenue gauntlet.

Mobs began to spread along Superior. Teenagers wrapped sweaters around their elbows and rammed plate glass windows of stores along the avenue, breaking them with a single thrust. "All you could hear was glass breaking," an eyewitness recalls. Gangs of looters and arsonists spread westward almost to Rockefeller Park, a buffer zone a mile away from Lakeview. At East 105th and Superior, close to Rockefeller Park, a block of buildings was burned to the ground. A store that Ahmed once had rented on Superior Avenue went up in flames, along with all the buildings next to it. Stores all along East 105th were looted. The violence spread all the way to St. Clair Avenue, more than a

mile north of Superior. Sporadically it broke out on the other side of Rockefeller Park, as far west as East 55th Street and including the troubled area of
Hough.

Patrol cars were dispatched to disperse looters, to answer calls of shootings, to pick up youths carrying gasoline cans or weapons. Often they had to
report back "gone on arrival" or "unable to locate." A heavy rainstorm
shortly after midnight offered hope of ending the violence, but the storm was
short lived. The looting and fire setting continued through the night. Fire
engines were brought in from all parts of the city and deployed in groups for
protection against the hindering mobs. Firemen sometimes arrived on the
scene to find hydrants had been opened, making it difficult to hook up hoses.
They faced gangs of youths throwing bottles and rocks at them; some reported sniper fire. Eventually, some fire crews refused to answer calls without a police escort. The next day Fire Chief William E. Barry reported that
the fire department had responded to between 50 and 60 legitimate fires in
the troubled area during the night, most of the fires occurring along Superior
Avenue east of Rockefeller Park. About 20 were "major" fires, involving two
or more buildings.[1]

Apart from those picked up as "suspicious persons" and those implicated
in the Glenville shooting, 28 Negroes were arrested during the night of July
23-24 in connection with the racial disturbances. Twenty-one were charged
with looting, one with malicious destruction of property, two with burglary,
and one with armed robbery. Three people related to one another were arrested near East 124th and Auburndale for carrying concealed weapons. All
but five of the 28 arrested were at least 20 years old. Five of those arrested
were women.

*   *   *

During the night, East Side hospitals, already overburdened with the victims of the Glenville gun battle, began to receive the casualties of the spread-
ing violence. Some were brought in mortally wounded.

About midnight, 19-year-old Eddie Roddick and three of his friends were
waiting for a bus at East 79th and St. Clair. Two cars drove up, according to
Roddick, each containing two white men. "They had pistols poking out of
the windows and they yelled racial insults at us." When one of the men fired
a shot, Roddick and his friends began running. Clifford Miller, a 22-year-old
Marine absent without leave from Camp Lejeune, ran 2 blocks along St. Clair
and then decided to stop. The white men got out of their cars, says Roddick;
one of them struck Miller on the head with his rifle, then another shot Miller
twice in the head with a pistol. (The coroner's examination revealed no
bruises, and only one gunshot wound.)

> The white men went back to their cars and started to drive off and we
> went to Clifford. We asked him if he was all right and one of us lifted
> his head. Then the white men got out of their cars again and one of us
> said "Let's get out of here. He's dead. We can't help him."

Then, said Roddick, the white men began to fire at him and his companions,
pursuing them until they escape into a nearby park. A patrol car, responding
to a report of the shooting, conveyed Miller to Mt. Sinai Hospital, where he
was pronounced dead on arrival.

Three days later the police picked up a white man and his two teenage sons as suspects in the shooting, but released them for want of evidence. The murder of Clifford Miller has never been solved.

*   *   *

James C. Haynes was a 30-year-old stock clerk who earned extra money as a custodian and guard in the apartment building in which he lived at 1270 East 83d Street. The building was close to Superior Avenue, and Haynes was aware of the looted and burning buildings at 105th and Superior, three-quarters of a mile to the east. Apprehensive about trouble in his own neighborhood, Haynes armed himself with a pistol. Around midnight, according to his father, a gang of youths attempted to enter the building; Haynes exchanged fire with them and the youths fled. (Others says Haynes merely fired into the air and the youths scattered.) Haynes returned to his apartment, picked up a shotgun, then walked downstairs and out of the building.

What happened next has never been clarified. One thing is clear: shots rang out. The body of James Haynes was later found in an alley behind 8203 Superior Avenue, riddled with shotgun wounds, another Negro fatality in Tuesday's long night of violence.

Around the corner from Haynes' apartment, a number of young black militants were gathered at the Afro Set, the craft shop and meeting place run by Harllel Jones. Early in the evening, Jones had given assurance to Law Director Clarence James and Councilman George Forbes that his followers would not participate in the violence. He himself was traveling through the troubled area with James and Forbes, helping them in their effort to restore peace and calm their fellow black citizens. Lyonel Jones (no relation to Harllel), director of the Legal Aid Society of Cleveland, was at the Afro Set to help keep the situation calm there. As a further precaution against trouble, James had stationed a Negro policeman at the building.

Police may have heard the pistol shots fired by Haynes, or they may have responded to a message, broadcast on patrol-car radios about 11:45 p.m., that two policemen were trapped in a building on East 82d and Superior and that Negro males were setting it afire. (The source and substance of that report are further unsolved elements in the episode.) In either case, very quickly there were several patrol cars at the scene.

According to Lyonel Jones, eight policement barged into the Afro Set, shot at the ceiling, and ordered the occupants to leave. A white captain ordered the Negro policeman whom James had stationed there to return to Fifth District headquarters. "Get your black ass out of here," he was overheard saying in response to the policeman's protests.

Then, say eyewitnesses, a patrol-car crew drove into a gas station, turned off the headlights, and began to fire in the direction of the apartment building where James Haynes lived. Another car, they say, drove into the alley behind Superior where Haynes was later found dead. Police believed they were being fired at; a patrol-car broadcast about 11:50 p.m. indicated two policemen were "pinned down" by snipers hiding in bushes in front of a funeral home near East 82d and Superior.

Law Director James, Councilman Forbes, and Harllel Jones arrived in a police car at 82d and Superior after the shooting had subsided. (James had been informed of the trouble there by the mayor's office in a phone conversation.) Another police vehicle, Car 351, was parked in front of the Afro Set. As James got out of the car, a group of young militants approached him in a state of excitement: "That's the car that did the shooting; that's the car that did the shooting [in the Afro Set] ," they said, indicating Car 351.

As James approached Car 351 to speak to its occupants, it pulled away from the curb and proceeded down Superior Avenue. James grabbed the microphone from his police car and radioed the following message: "Car 351, this is the Law Director; return to the scene on Superior that you just left." Car 351 kept going, slowed down momentarily, then sped up again as James repeated his message. Then it turned into a side street.

James and Forbes got into the police car and ordered the driver to pursue Car 351 with the siren on. They turned where Car 351 turned, but the patrol car was not in sight. James called the radio dispatcher: "This is the Law Director in 8C. Will you locate Car 351?" He heard the dispatcher broadcast the message: "Car 351: your location?" There was no answer. Then James thought he saw 351 ahead of them, running without lights on. He pursued the car, siren still screaming. As he drew near, Car 351 slowed to a stop in front of him. The headlights came on. "Car 351," James radioed, "this is the Law Director right behind you. Please get out of your car and come back to me."

When the three policemen in Car 351 approached, James asked one of them, a sergeant, if he had heard him at 82d and Superior telling him to stop and return to the scene. The sergeant replied, "No; we didn't hear you." Raising his helmet, he added: "You know, we can't hear to well with these things on." Another said: "We've got the radio turned down and did not hear you call." Why, James wanted to know, would they have the radio turned down when there was all this trouble in the city? James found their answers unconvincing.

Then James asked the sergeant to accompany him back to 82d and Superior while the other officers followed in Car 351. (Only when they arrived back at the Afro Set did James realize that one of the other officers was a captain, and thus in charge of Car 351.) As they rode back, James told the sergeant about the complaints of residents that Car 351 had done unnecessary shooting. The sergeant denied the claims, saying Car 351 had just arrived on the scene.

When they reached the Afro Set, James learned that a dead body has been found in the alley behind Lakeview. He and others examined the body of Haynes, then James asked the police captain, "How did this happen?" "I don't know," said the captain; "we had just come up." James asked what had happened to the Negro policeman he had stationed at the Afro Set. The captain admitted that he had sent the officer to Fifth District headquarters, but denied that the man ever mentioned that he had been under orders from Law Director James.

Residents of the area were giving James their versions of what had happened. They told him about the patrol car parked at the gas station firing at the apartment building on 83d Street. One confirmed that spent shells were lying on the ground at the gas station. A police photographer had arrived, and James sent him to take pictures of the shells. Then James and others examined the exterior of the apartment building. "That building has been riddled with bullets," he told the policemen. "How did this happen?" The captain and the sergeant again replied that they had no knowledge of the matter since they had just arrived. People in the crowd said they had seen a patrol car shooting at the building. Concerned that the shooting might have produced casualties, James, the policemen and others entered the building to examine it. In a second-floor apartment they found that high-powered bullets had gone through windows and torn through the walls, leaving gaping holes where they lodged. There were holes above the beds of two small children who had been sleeping when the shooting started.

City officials later promised an investigation of the shootings near East 82d and Superior, probing for instances of police misconduct. If the investigation took place, the conclusions have not been made public.

* * *

Through the long night of July 23-24, 1968, Mayor Stokes and top officials at City Hall struggled with the decisions to be made about how to cope with the violence in Cleveland. They were hampered by inadequate and confusing information about the violence as it happened, and by the lack of contingency planning for such emergencies.

When he learned of the outbreak of shooting from Safety Director Joseph McManamon about 8:30 p.m., Stokes decided to meet with McManamon and others at Sixth District police headquarters, then changed his mind and moved the meeting to City Hall. When Stokes arrived at City Hall about 9 p.m., officials were monitoring the police radio and McManamon had a direct hookup for talking to police at the scene of the Glenville gun battle. The number of patrol cars that had rushed to the Lakeview-Auburndale area, the tension of the situation there, the lack of coordination and measured response, made it difficult to assess what was happening. It was similarly difficult to get a clear picture of events as the violence spread. An aide described the situation at City Hall as "totally confusing."

> It sounded a lot worse than it was. It sounded like the city was burning down and that people were being shot over the whole city. . . . In fact, there were a couple of isolated shootings that were not related at all. They are the normal shootings that you would have.

He and others report that frequently during the night the police radio carried rumors and false reports that exaggerated the extent of the violence.

Partly to rectify this, Mayor Stokes sent Law Director Clarence James into the troubled area to act as his personal observer and reporter.

Perhaps buoyed by its success after the assassination of Martin Luther King, the Stokes administration found itself inadequately prepared to handle the violence of July 23. Control of the situation was, in the beginning stages, left to police on the scene, and, as Stokes was later to admit, Cleveland police were inadequately trained and supplied to cope with urban guerrilla warfare.[2] According to Maj. Gen. Sylvester Del Corso, Adjutant General of the Ohio National Guard, he had tried to get the Stokes administration to discuss measures for handling racial disturbances but had been rebuffed.

By 9:15 p.m., Stokes had decided that the situation might get beyond the control of local forces before the night was over. He called Gov. James A. Rhodes, who was attending the National Governors Conference in Cincinnati, to inform him of the situation. The Governor immediately called General

Del Corso, who was in Akron, and told him to report to Stokes. Within a few minutes, Rhodes left for his home in Columbus to monitor the disturbances from there, General Del Corso was on his way to Cleveland, and the Ohio National Guard had been placed on alert.

In addition to determining the level of force needed to control the violence, Mayor Stokes knew that he would have to inform the public of the situation, to avoid misunderstanding and panic and to keep people out of the troubled area. After talking to the Governor, the mayor went down the street from City Hall to the television studies of WKYC. There he taped a special announcement to be used by WKYC and distributed in copy to other Cleveland television and radio stations. Many Clevelanders, watching a televised baseball game between the Cleveland Indians and the Baltimore Orioles, got the first news of the violence when Mayor Stokes interrupted the broadcast shortly before 11 p.m.:

> We've had a bad situation here tonight but as of this time we have the situation controlled. But we do need badly the help of every citizen at this time, particularly in the Lakeview-Superior Avenue area. Stay at home and cooperate with the police. Go home if you are on the streets; if you are at home, stay inside and keep your doors locked so that we can contain the situation.

Later this message was broadcast over the civil defense network.

General Del Corso arrived at City Hall about 11 p.m. and began deliberations with Stokes on the use of National Guard troops. Shortly after midnight the mayor signed a proclamation, addressed to General Del Corso, formally requesting National Guard assistance. "Law enforcement agencies under my jurisdiction can no longer adequately cope with the riotous situation that exists in the City of Cleveland," the proclamation began.

General Del Corso communicated with other National Guard officials, then emerged at 1:10 a.m. to report on the situation to the press. A total of 15,400 Ohio National Guardsmen had been mobilized, he announced, including 2,600 from the Cleveland area. The 107th Armored Cavalry Regiment in Cleveland had 1,800 Guardsmen to assist police. Seven hundred Guardsmen undergoing summer training at Camp Perry, 60 miles from Cleveland, would be brought into the city. By daylight, General Del Corso estimated, there would be 2,600 National Guard troops in Cleveland, ready to be deployed.

Still, there had been no decision about how, when, and how many Guardsmen should be deployed in the troubled area. It would take some time to get troops combat ready. In the meantime, Mayor Stokes was trying to keep abreast of the situation in the troubled area, talking frequently on the telephone with Clarence James and with black community spokesmen like Baxter Hill and Harllel Jones, who were also working to calm things down. A young black nationalist was in the mayor's office, occasionally leaving the office to make telephone calls of his own to friends, urging them to "cool it." About 2 a.m., a number of black leaders met with Stokes in his office to help him assess the situation.

By 3 a.m., when General Del Corso notified him that he had a number of troops ready for deployment, Mayor Stokes had decided that the time had come to use the National Guard. Two hundred Guardsmen, together with 24 Jeeps and other military vehicles, were sent to the troubled area to patrol the streets. To each of the Jeeps were assigned three Guardsmen and one Cleveland policeman. About 4:30 a.m. the police, on orders from the mayor, were instructed to report any sniper activity to the National Guard. Looters and arsonists, said the police-radio announcement, "are to be arrested by police or National Guard without the use of deadly force." Half an hour later, the police heard another announcement on their patrol-car radios: All vacations and holidays are canceled; all personnel will work 12-hour shifts.

As dawn arrived amid a drizzle, smoke still rose from gutted buildings along Superior Avenue. Police continued to receive reports of looting and of sporadic gunfire in areas of the East Side. But the worst of the violence had abated. Cleveland, for the time being, was under control.

*   *   *

From the history of racial disturbances in Cleveland and other American cities, Clevelanders, on the morning of July 24, 1968, had every reason to expect that more trouble lay ahead. If past patterns were repeated, more violence would flare at nightfall. The authorities had to devise a strategy to cope with it.

More than 100 leaders of the black community gathered at City Hall about 8:30 a.m. to meet with Mayor Stokes. The attendance at this meeting was entirely black; not even the white members of the mayor's staff were permitted to take part. Many at the meeting had been up all night, assisting in City Hall or walking the streets, attempting to quell the violence.

Stokes opened the meeting with his assessment of the situation, then called for discussion on how best to handle it. A number of options were available to the mayor: He could impose a curfew, strengthen police and National Guard units in the troubled area, or use various combinations of force such as placing National Guard in the area and not police. Many at the meeting were concerned that if police were allowed to remain in the area, there would be further shooting. They feared that black nationalists would be made fidgety by the continued presence of the police and would begin shooting, or that if police were allowed to remain in the area, they would seek revenge for their three comrades who were killed the night before. Several spoke in opposition to a curfew, noting that if it were applied to just one area it would be resented by the citizens of that area and would not prevent outsiders from coming into the area and beginning violence again.

The meeting at City Hall produced no real consensus, and Mayor Stokes revealed no plans of his own. When the meeting broke up about 10 a.m., he retired to his office to discuss strategies with his staff, while about 20 of the participants in the meeting, most of them militants, adjourned to the Auditorium Hotel to continue discussions.

An hour later Stokes addressed a press conference originally scheduled for 9:30 a.m. He attributed Tuesday night's violence to "a gang who will meet the full measure of the law" and described the present situation on the East Side as "quiet."

> Security measures are being maintained with a minimum number of National Guardsmen on our streets and a sizeable force in ready reserve should they be needed. I have met with Negro leadership at City Hall and they have joined me in an all-out effort to make sure that Cleveland's night of terror will not turn into a riot. We are constantly

re-evaluating the situation and assure that this city will not be governed by hoodlums.

The mayor indicated that he had not yet decided upon a strategy for Wednesday evening.

Early in the afternoon the group of militants returned from the Auditorium Hotel to City Hall. Now they presented a definite proposal to the mayor: They would go back into the community and try to bring it under control themselves, preventing looting, burning, and additional loss of life. They wanted a period of time to attempt this; if it did not work, Stokes could choose a different strategy. Stokes listened. He still made no commitment.

This was not the first time such a proposal had been suggested to Stokes. Bertram Gardner, who had spent the night on the streets, proposed such a course to the Mayor in a conversation about 7:30 a.m. Gardner wanted Stokes to take the police and Guard out of the area, while Gardner sent about 200 or 250 blacks into the community to try to calm feelings. He wanted only about 6 hours: from about 11 a.m. to about 5 p.m. At the 8:30 a.m. meeting, others had proposed a similar course.

About midafternoon, Stokes discussed the idea with others in a small meeting in his office. Richard Greene, director of the Community Development Department, endorsed the proposal. He felt that the black community ought to be given a chance to "pull itself together." Councilman George Forbes expressed confidence that the strategy would work. Not all were convinced. General Del Corso expressed serious reservations about the wisdom of the proposal.

When the mayor made his decision, he did not make it rashly. He had had the benefit of numerous opinions and arguments for and against competing strategies. Some options, like the curfew, had been seen as fraught with difficulties. Stokes had heard compelling arguments about the volatile situation that would be created by the continuing presence of white law enforcement officers in the black community. The "all black" strategy appeared to be the only rational policy to reduce bloodshed. In accepting it, Stokes knew he was taking a calculated risk. There would be safeguards, however. He accepted the suggestion by Richard Greene that Negro policemen function in the area as well as the black leaders. He would also station police and the National Guard around the perimeter of the area, so that they could respond quickly if trouble did arise.

Though the decision was not his alone, Stokes had to assume full responsibility for it. It was a novel strategy, one that a white mayor would have had greater difficulty in instrumenting. It was Stokes' rapport with the Negro community that brought forth the proposal in the first place and that now gave hope that it would work.

At 4:15 p.m., Mayor Stokes released a detailed plan for Wednesday night. About 6 square miles of the city were to be cordoned off until 7 a.m., Thursday morning. The southern boundary would be Euclid Avenue, eastward from East 55th Street. The northern boundary would be Superior Avenue, from East 55th to Rockefeller Park, then along the park's eastern edge up to St. Clair, eastward along St. Clair (with a small section north of it) to the city line adjoining East Cleveland. This perimeter was to be patrolled by units of three National Guardsmen and one police officer, beginning at 7 p.m. The National

Guard was to retain a mobile reserve to deploy within the cordoned area should serious trouble arise.

"Normal patrol within the cordoned-off area," said the memo, "will be restricted to regular Cleveland police as directed by the Safety Director. National Guard troops will be committed to the area only if needed."

Though the memorandum did not mention that only Negro policemen would be allowed in the area, Mayor Stokes spelled out this provision in a press conference at 4:45 p.m.

> There will only be Negro policemen and possibly a Negro sheriff in the area guarding the people. . . . There will be 109 [individuals] who will represent the groups themselves and about five hundred persons who are familiar with this situation will be in the area.

All white nonresidents, including newsmen, were to be kept from the area. The mayor repeated that it was important for people to stay home and off the streets. He made two further announcements: that the sale of liquor in Cuyahoga County (embracing Cleveland) had been stopped for 72 hours beginning at 11 a.m., Wednesday; that four emergency centers had been set up in East Side churches and community centers to provide food and shelter for those displaced by Tuesday night's disturbances.

The Reverend DeForest Brown, director of the Hough Area Development Corporation, was named spokesman for the Mayor's Committee which was to patrol the streets that night. Said Brown:

> We, out of our concern, have accepted the responsibility to restore law and order out of a chaotic situation. Leaders will be out talking to the black community about its responsibility to itself.

The mayor had made his decision. On Wednesday evening black control was established for the black community.

REFERENCES

1. Barry's figures were far in excess of those reported by others. In a summary report on the violence, issued Aug. 9, the mayor's office said there were 24 reported fires during the first 24 hours of violence, of which 14 were set by vandals, 1 was a rekindle of an earlier fire, 6 were false alarms, and 4 were fires unrelated to the disturbance.
2. In addition to lacking weapons equal in power to those the snipers used, the police lacked armored vehicles and had to commandeer trucks from Brinks, Inc., and rush them to the Lakeview area.

Chapter 4

LAW AND ORDER

Wednesday, July 24, passed in heat and mugginess, the mugginess fed by light rainshowers that swept over the city at noontime. Through the day the police responded to sporadic calls of looting and of looters hawking stolen goods on street corners. They closed bars that were violating the liquor ban and investigated rumors of looting and violence planned for Wednesday evening. Here and there merchants boarded up the windows of their stores or carted away valuable merchandise. (Later there were claims that some merchants took what they could, then encouraged looters to take the rest, figuring they would get adequate recompense from their insurance companies.) As 7 p.m. approached, the roving patrols of police and Guardsmen retreated to the perimeter of the cordoned area. There was a thunderstorm early in the evening, but at dusk the sky was clearing and the heat and mugginess lingered.

The Negro leaders carried the message from City Hall back to their communities, meeting with small groups to explain the evening's strategy and to organize for effective peacekeeping. At the office of Pride, Inc., on St. Clair, Wilbur Grattan, a black nationalist associated with the New Republic of Africa, addressed a group of about 30, most of whom were members of the Circle of African Unity. Grattan had spent much of the previous night in peacekeeping and most of the day in the meetings that led to Mayor Stokes' decision to exercise black control in the black community. He described what had been discussed during those meetings, praised the bold policy that had been adopted, then turned to matters of organization for the evening. After being told by Grattan that they would receive orange arm bands labeled "The Mayor's Committee," the group worked out the problems of geographic assignments for each of them. Baxter Hill, director of Pride, Inc., closed the meeting in his office with a reminder of the significance of the responsibilities they were about to undertake.

Hill stayed on for awhile at the Pride office, which was to be the headquarters for the peacekeeping operation through the night. (A Negro radio station broadcast the telephone number of Pride frequently during the evening, urging listeners to report crowds, looting, or other indications of trouble.) The expected 500 peace patrols were to be divided into four "companies," headed by Harllel Jones, William (Sonny) Denton of the United Youth Council, and two from Baxter Hill's organization: Benjamin Lloyd and Ronald Turner.

While the Negro leaders were hastily organizing their peacekeeping force, the Cleveland Police Department was preparing for its role in the troubled area. White policemen were assigned to work with National Guardsmen patrolling the perimeter of the cordoned area. At Fifth District headquarters, situated within the area, police climbed aboard military trucks and joked about being back in the Army. American Legionnaires served them coffee. About 100 Negro policemen (out of a total of 165 Negro officers in the 2,200-man police force) were assigned to patrol the cordoned area, using 21 patrol cars. Negroes on the county sheriff's staff were assigned to help them. White police, it was understood, would enter the area only if the Negro officers needed additional assistance.

*   *   *

The sky had not yet darkened when firetrucks were called to East 105th and Superior to extinguish fires that were rekindles (accidental or intentional) of burned-out stores. A crowd gathered to watch. Nearby, some Negro businessmen were removing merchandise from their stores and, when the owner of a record store left, some who had stood watching walked in and helped themselves to odds and ends he had left behind.

The crowd at the intersection had swelled to several hundred when members of the Mayor's Committee arrived to disperse them. A few of the peace patrols talked to the crowd in front of the record store. Most stood in the middle of the intersection, imploring the crowd to go home. A rumor was afloat that a child was trapped in the basement of a burning pawnshop. Firemen said they had searched the basement and no child was there. Noting that such a thing could happen, the Mayor's Committee pleaded with parents to take their children home.

Children stayed on. Some of them found clothing in the back of a store that had been nearly gutted the night before, and soon a crowd was surging toward the rear of the store. After considerable cajoling, the Mayor's Committee managed to discourage the looting. But the technique of talking to the crowd from the middle of the intersection was not dispersing the people. Walter Beach, Ron Lucas, Baxter Hill, and Harllel Jones decided that if they were going to be effective, they had to walk among the crowd and talk to the people, two or three at a time. Though it took more than an hour to disperse the crowd, the technique worked.

Through the night, teams of peace patrols drove up and down the commercial streets of the area, stopping wherever four or more people were standing around, pleading with them to disperse. Occasionally members of the Mayor's Committee stood in front of stores where windows had been broken or iron gates torn down, directly confronting the potential looters. This technique could not be wholly effective, for the Mayor's Committee lacked the manpower for permanent guards at every commercial establishment. Potential looters, some of them professionals, lurked in the shadows, sometimes for hours, waiting for the peace patrols to leave the scene. Days later they would be seen hawking stolen goods on street corners. Occasionally a looter broke into a store, setting off the burglar alarm, then hid nearby until someone came to investigate, turned off the alarm, and walked away. Most looters made off with what they could carry, but some filled automobiles with merchandise.

The Mayor's Committee observed adults, including women, among the potential and actual looters, but teenagers gave them the most trouble. Roving bands of teenagers usually were the first to break into a store, then proved unresponsive to the appeals of the peace patrols. "We couldn't control the kids," Walter Burks, executive assistant to the Mayor, recalls. "We would tell them to stop and they would walk away and you would get into your car to drive someplace else and you would drive back and they were right back with their hands in [the windows of a looted store]." Some of the troublesome youths, says Burks, were not more than 10 years old. The next day Mayor Stokes ascribed most of the trouble Wednesday night to "roving bands of young people generally between the ages of fourteen and seventeen."

An observer who accompanied members of the Mayor's Committee on their patrols recalls that some were particularly effective in their work. Harllel Jones, a young militant, wiry and ordinarily soft-spoken, dispersed a crowd at 123d and St. Clair that had gathered in front of a furniture store that had been broken into. "At 105th and Massey," the observer adds, "Harllel dispersed perhaps the potentially most dangerous crowd of about two hundred people. It took him about twenty to twenty-five minutes." Like the other militants who were particularly effective Wednesday night, Harllel Jones succeeded by making eloquent pleas to the pride of the black community. "If there was one man who stands out as having done the most effective job possible of maintaining peace," said the observer, "it was Harllel Jones."[1]

Noticeable by their absence were the clergymen and other moderate and middle-class Negro leaders. Though a number of them had participated in the meetings at City Hall, few were on the streets Wednesday night and their effectiveness was limited. Had more moderates helped out, the members of the peace patrol felt, the sporadic looting might have been prevented entirely.

White policemen appeared in the cordoned area over the protests of the Mayor's Committee. When a pawnbroker's window was broken at East 101st and St. Clair, white policemen responded to the call. They ignored requests of the peace patrol to leave. Similar incidents occurred elsewhere. At East 123d and St. Clair, an observer recalls, an alarm went off in a furniture store.

> All of a sudden National Guardsmen and white policemen, who apparently had been stationed in East Cleveland, appeared on the scene. They started backing up toward the buildings as if they were actually in a state of emergency. Nothing had occurred and, fortunately, the Law Director arrived on the scene.

Law Director James talked to the white officers, and they left.

* * *

The reaction of some white policemen to Mayor Stokes' strategy of black control was made clear to those monitoring the police radio Wednesday night.

This came in response to a report of a heart-attack case within the cordoned area: "White or nigger? Send the Mayor's Committee."

When a report was broadcast that a child had fallen off a second-floor porch, the return call came: "Tell the Mayor's Committee to handle it."

When the police dispatcher requested cars to respond to a fire call, an anonymous voice suggested that Mayor Stokes "go p...on it." Responses to other calls included "F . . . that nigger Mayor!"

At the Fifth District headquarters, the heavily guarded bastion within the troubled area, police responded in a fury of curses and epithets, directed toward Stokes and Safety Director McManamon, when told they could not carry rifles while patrolling the perimeter of the cordoned area. A policeman there, delivering a monolog to a bystander on what is "wrong" with Negroes, gave this assessment of Mayor Stokes: "You need a sheepdog to lead sheep; you don't have a sheep lead other sheep."2

The tension at Fifth District headquarters lasted through the evening. Two television newsmen who entered the building were grabbed from behind by a commanding officer, pushed through the building, and thrown out into the parking lot where other policemen shouted at them abusively. After appealing to another commanding officer they were let back in, and ultimately the first officer apologized for ejecting them.

*   *   *

At a press conference late the next morning, Mayor Stokes pronounced the strategy for Wednesday night a qualified success.

> It is our considered opinion that we made significant headway last night in bringing to an end the violence and lawlessness that has occurred on · our East Side. No one was killed or shot or seriously injured during the night.

Stokes admitted that there had been trouble; he reported that 3 fires had been set, 36 stores looted, and 13 persons arrested in the troubled area.3 "Most of the trouble," he said, "was caused by young teenagers, roving in small bands." He expressed thanks to the National Guard patrolling the perimeter, the Negro policemen working within the area, and especially the 300 members of the Mayor's Committee "who patrolled the troubled areas until dawn to keep things cool." He announced that bus service and garbage pickup had resumed in the cordoned area and that city workers had begun to tear down dangerously damaged buildings. He emphasized, however, that more trouble could be expected.

Earlier in the morning, Stokes had met with Negro leaders at City Hall. During that meeting the resentment over the limited participation of moderate Negro leaders in the peacekeeping was brought into the open. It was generally agreed that the peace patrols had been only partially effective; the arson and looting had not been completely curbed. Changes were needed: A curfew now might help remove the gangs from the streets; more cars equipped with radios were needed; more sound trucks would help; and broken windows should be boarded before nightfall.

While the Negro leaders continued their discussion in the City Council chamber, the mayor addressed the press conference. There he announced a change in strategy: The National Guard, he said, was being brought into the area to protect stores against looting. This change in strategy, like others he made that Thursday, was to haunt Carl Stokes for weeks to come, for it provided an indication to his critics that he had given in to pressure from others or conceded the failure of his Wednesday-night strategy. Throughout the ensuing controversy, Stokes would maintain that the strategy had succeeded because it had prevented bloodshed, and he valued life over property. Changes in the strategy, he argued, became appropriate after tempers had cooled in the black community and the protection of property could be safely entrusted to white law enforcement officers.

One of the first to criticize the mayor was Councilman Leo Jackson, whose district includes part of Glenville and who is said to represent the views of older, established Negro residents. "If you want to say what happened last night—no shootings, no sniping—was a success, then it was," Jackson told a reporter. "But if you consider the looting, the destruction, the breaking of windows, the wholesale gutting of buildings, last night's activities were a total failure."

Businessmen whose stores were victimized Wednesday night were bitterly critical of the mayor's policy. The white owner of a looted clothing store drove to the scene about 1 a.m. and could not get out of his car because of an attacking mob. A Negro policeman ordered him out of the area for his own safety. At the perimeter he pleaded with National Guardsmen and police for help, but was told there was nothing they could do. The owner of a looted furniture store got the same response from police at Fifth District headquarters. A partner in a drycleaning chain, two of whose stores had been looted the previous night, had his main plant looted of clothing Wednesday night—half a million dollars' worth, he estimated. "We're wiped out," he said bitterly. "We couldn't get help. That means 70 people out of work—70 families without incomes."

White policemen were openly critical of the mayor's Wednesday-night strategy. A 30-year-old patrolman angrily submitted his resignation. When Police Chief Michael Blackwell called the mayor's strategy "a brilliant idea," there were murmurings that Blackwell, a 42-year veteran of the force, was a traitor to his department and a politician protecting himself.

Gen. Del Corso, who had argued for much stronger measures Wednesday night, declined to criticize the mayor.

> I made my suggestions but the Mayor made the decision and I am sure he did a lot of soul-searching all day. We're here to assist and cooperate with the Mayor. He wanted to use this means [citizen-patrols] and it is beginning to be productive. It is proving successful.

It came as a shock to City Hall when, on August 9, Gen. Del Corso told the Ohio Crime Commission that Stokes had "surrendered to black revolutionaries."

That same day, after the Stokes administration presented a summary of events to city councilmen and to the press, Council President James V. Stanton, considered by many to be a leading contender for the office occupied by Carl Stokes, joined in the criticism. "I find no moral grounds," he said, "for taking duly constituted law enforcement away from the families and property of that area regardless of any justification by the Administration that there was no loss of life." Stanton's charge brought a rejoinder from Safety Director Joseph McManamon. "He can't say that," McManamon retorted, "unless he means that Negro policemen aren't duly constituted officers." He added that the concentration of Negro policemen on Wednesday evening added up to the normal number of police in the area.

In the days following the Wednesday-night disturbances, support for the mayor's strategy, sometimes in the form of newspaper advertisements, came from civil rights groups, religious and charitable organizations, liberal political groups, and from Cleveland educators, industrial leaders, and other prominent citizens. A professional polling organization found that 59 percent of its respondents supported the mayor's strategy; 14 percent criticized it; the rest were uncertain.

*   *   *

Four hundred National Guardsmen moved into the cordoned area on Thursday morning to help Cleveland police control the sporadic but persistent looting. Police were also kept busy through the day enforcing the liquor ban and tracking down rumors of violence threatened for Thursday night. Teenagers employed by Pride, Inc., carted away debris from damaged buildings.

Meanwhile, Mayor Stokes pondered a strategy for Thursday night, questioning whether to impose a curfew and whether to allow National Guardsmen and white policemen in the area after dark. Early in the afternoon he took a walk, touring the streets of Glenville for the first time since the trouble began July 23, urging residents to keep their children at home Thursday night. At 4 p.m. he met with Baxter Hill and other Negro leaders at the office of Pride, Inc. He sought their counsel on a strategy for Thursday night. Most agreed that additional enforcement was necessary. With some reluctance, stemming more from concern for the unpredictable behavior of white policemen than of black nationalists, they agreed that National Guardsmen and white policemen should be allowed to remain in the area after nightfall.

Mayor Stokes announced his decision at a press conference about 6:30 p.m. A curfew would be imposed on the cordoned area, beginning at 9 p.m. and extending to 6:30 a.m., Friday morning. The National Guard would stay in the area,[4] and no policemen would be constrained from entering the area.

Though the announcement was carried on television and radio stations, it was a late-hour decision that caught many unprepared. Some police first learned of the curfew from a police radio broadcast 20 minutes before the curfew was to begin. Sound trucks were sent into the area to announce the curfew, but did not reach some neighborhoods until 10:30 p.m. People were still walking the streets after 10 p.m. and some businesses were still open. A reporter saw a National Guard unit still encamped in Rockefeller Park at 10:30 p.m.

Stokes had disbanded the Mayor's Committee, but a number of Negro leaders worked Thursday night to keep the peace, patrolling the area in nine cars.

Though the peacekeeping operation on Thursday night was massive, according with the wishes of those who had urged strong enforcement, it was not 100 percent successful. At a predawn press conference, John Little, the mayor's executive secretary, gave a summary report of the night's violence. A major fire had occurred on East 55th Street; there had been four minor fires, of which two were described as "flareups" toward the eastern end of Superior Avenue. Thirty people had been arrested: one for attempted arson, two for looting, the rest for curfew violations. Guardsmen had been sent to disperse more than 100 youths roaming the streets in the southeast corner of Cleveland, far from the cordoned area. There were no reports of sniping.

Friday was a time of relative calm. There were indications the community was returning to normal. The liquor ban was lifted in the suburbs of Cuyahoga County, and Mayor Stokes was expected to approve a lifting of the ban in Cleveland the next morning. (He did.) The Friday-night curfew was delayed until midnight, permitting residents of the cordoned area to attend a Cleveland Indians baseball game.

For the forces of law and order, Friday was not completely a dull day. That afternoon, an army of about 35 policemen and 100 National Guardsmen, equipped with rifles, shotguns, and tear gas, surrounded the Esquire

Hotel at 10602 Superior Avenue. They were there in response to a tip that a number of snipers involved in Tuesday night's shootout were hiding in the hotel. A police bullhorn urged the men to give themselves up. The episode turned seriocomic when three unarmed teenagers emerged from the hotel. Nothing incriminating was found in their rooms but they were arrested anyway, on suspicion of possessing stolen property (a radio, a camera, and two adding machines).

On Friday night, at the Afro Set, Harllel Jones and six youths were charged by police with violating the midnight curfew. The police searched Jones and said they found brass knuckles in his pockets; without a warrant they searched his car and claimed to find a .38-caliber revolver. (Police later changed their report to read that they found brass knuckles. The court dismissed the case against Jones on September 16 on grounds that the search was illegal.) Mayor Stokes, having gotten word of the arrest, arrived while Jones was being held, assured the watching crowd that no harm would befall Jones, and assigned a Negro policeman to accompany Jones through the arresting process. After the mayor left, according to Jones' followers, police kicked down the door of the Afro Set, gassed the shop, broke the front window, and damaged articles in the store.[5]

There were few other incidents of violence Friday night, and on Saturday morning Mayor Stokes pronounced the crisis past. National Guardsmen had begun to leave the area. Police were restored to 8-hour shifts. There would be no curfew Saturday night. The mayor, other City Hall officials, and hundreds of policemen went to a Catholic church to attend a memorial service for the three policemen slain Tuesday night.

Not all the tensions had subsided. Cleveland had not seen the last of violence.

* * *

Julius Boros and Charles Ray were television cameramen from Chicago, assigned by the National Broadcasting Co. to accompany two news teams covering the disturbances in Cleveland. They had been dispatched to Cleveland shortly after trouble broke out Tuesday night, July 22.

Boros and Ray were still on assignment in Cleveland Saturday night. At about 2:30 a.m. (Sunday morning), a disturbance broke out at the entrance to the Haddam Hotel on Euclid Avenue, a block away from Fifth District police headquarters at Chester and East 107th Street. According to eyewitnesses, a young black man was arguing with the hotel's night watchman. The watchman pulled a gun, fired a warning shot into the ground, then struck the Negro on the head with the gun. Bars and nightclubs along Euclid were closing, and a large crowd began to gather at the scene. As police also started to arrive, the Negro involved in the altercation got on a bus and left the area.

In the crowd of Negroes was 19-year-old Jerome Pritchard, who had been yelling at the watchman and who now, according to police, shouted obscenities at them and urged the crowd to attack the police. Pritchard was later charged with carrying a knife and inciting a riot. Observers say police jumped on Pritchard and began to beat him. Others were being attacked. A bystander said that, without provocation, a policeman struck him in the jaw with the butt of a rifle, chipping three of his teeth.

Boros and Ray, who had been sitting at Fifth District police headquarters awaiting newsworthy developments, rushed to the scene when they got word of the disturbance a block away. With other members of the NBC crews they went in separate cars, and Ray's crew got there first.

According to Charles Ray, a 40-year-old photographer who had covered racial disturbances before, the scene was "tumultuous." Policemen were swarming into the area, patrol cars were blocking traffic, and crowds were standing on the corners of 105th and Euclid. Ray took wide-angle shots of the scene, then moved toward the other side of the street to film a ruckus going on there. As he raised his camera to his eye, says Ray, more than a dozen policemen rushed at him, shouting "Get that camera!" A plainclothesman grabbed the camera, raised it as through to smash it to the ground, but ran across the street with it. The other police turned away as Ray demanded his camera back. He found a lieutenant in the middle of the street, showed him his press credentials, and demanded the return of his property. The lieutenant shoved him away, saying "Get out of here; don't bother me."

About five policemen, Ray recalls, grabbed him, pushed him against a wall, pinned his arms, and began a search. One took his light meter, another examined his wallet. A policeman took off Ray's glasses, folded them, and stuck them in the pocket of Ray's coat. Then all began hitting him.

> It looked like a football huddle . . . Everyone was pounding on me at once, and fists were flying in my face. Feet were kicking me in the back and buttocks and I was trying to avoid getting hit in the groin, so I doubled up . . . and put my hands and my arms over my head to protect my face and head as best I could.

The police pulled Ray from the ground, punched and kicked him some more, then dragged him to a police station wagon and threw him inside. Ray's foot was caught in the door as it slammed, trapped but uninjured, and police refused to help him dislodge the foot. "You dirty bastard, we hope your foot is broken," said one of the policemen who drove him to Fifth District headquarters. At the police station, says Ray, he was rabbit punched by police before being thrown into a cell.

Julius Boros, a 36-year-old cameraman who had worked many years as a photographer in his native Hungary, arrived at 105th and Euclid after Charles Ray. He had to walk half a block to the intersection because patrol cars and other automobiles were backed up on 105th. Near the intersection an NBC soundman yelled to him that Ray had had his camera stolen and was being beaten by police. "Don't go up there," he warned.

But Boros kept going. He did not see Ray, but across the street he saw police roughly handling about 12 Negroes lined against a wall with their hands up. Ray estimates he stepped 5 feet into the street from the curb; there he began to film a "general shot" of the activity. Suddenly there was a policeman running in his direction, hatless, hands held high, face contorted in rage, screaming "You son of a bitch!" Boros turned, thinking someone else was meant, but the policeman pounced on him, grabbed the camera, threw it to the ground, and started kicking the cameraman.

Boros fell to his knees. Half-a-dozen police, Boros estimates, rushed over and began kicking and punching him and jabbing him with their rifle butts. They picked him up, dragged him a few feet, and resumed to pummeling. The next few moments were to be crucial ones. According to Boros, he was dazed, his eyes were closed, and as he began to sink once more under the pummeling, he feared he would lose consciousness. He grabbed at anything that would support him. He had hold of a policeman's shoulder with his left hand, he recalls, then the policeman's belt as he slid toward the ground. His right hand grabbed an object and, when his eyes responded to the tactile signal, Boros found he was holding the policeman's gun by the barrel.

That is how Boros describes those few moments, and it is doubtful whether Cleveland policemen ever will believe his account. When he realized what had happened, says Boros, he said, "Officer, here is your gun." As he reached out his hand, the policemen on top of him became aware of the gun and began shouting. The gun was grabbed away. Then the officer who had assaulted Boros originally put his face close to the cameraman's and screamed, "You are under arrest!"

The beating then became ferocious. Boros was dragged behind a patrol car on 105th Street and pummeled as he lay prone on the ground. "God help me, please," he cried out. "Please help me." It was then, for the first time, that he noticed Charles Ray, undergoing beating nearby, unable to assist him. Boros was then thrown to the floor in the rear of a patrol car. He recalls nothing of the trip to Fifth District headquarters; cold water, slammed in his face at the police station, brought him back to awareness. He remembers policemen beating him and swearing at him as he was led from the garage into the building. In the hallway he appealed to a high-ranking officer for help, but the officer ignored him. At the window where he was fingerprinted, says Boros, the policeman who had originally assaulted him stood 3 or 4 feet away, lit matches, and threw them at him. When another policeman struck him with a rifle, Boros screamed out in terror: "Please help me. Don't kill me here!" Boros spoke briefly to Charles Ray, locked in a cell, as he was led to a cell of his own. There he found running water to slake his thirst and wash his bloody face. In pain, suffering nausea, Boros asked police officers passing his cell to get him a doctor. "Not now," they said.

Law Director Clarence James learned of the trouble at Euclid and 105th from Walter Burks, executive assistant to Mayor Stokes. When he arrived there, all was quiet. In another telephone conversation with Burks, James learned of the arrest of the NBC cameramen. James went to pick up Councilman George Forbes, and both went to Fifth District headquarters. The police station was, by James' recollection, a nervous armed camp "ringed with police officers, shotguns, and machineguns." A policeman guarding the door from the garage was reluctant to let them in, despite James' position as city law director. After vehement protest they eventually got in, and James began to notice peculiarities. He passed through a room containing four or five captains and three lieutenants, an unusual number of high-ranking officers. An inspector said they were there taking care of "platoon business." No Negro policemen were in sight. Few patrolmen were wearing badges; a sergeant and a captain were wearing theirs, but they were unnumbered.

When Forbes and James saw Boros, his face "a mass of blood and puffed up," James ordered him taken to Lakeside Hospital.

A few Negro policemen came into Fifth District headquarters, and James asked one of them to accompany him to a nearby coffee shop. Over coffee the Negro policeman told him that black suspects were being beaten at the

Fifth that night. The paddy wagon would be backed up to the garage door, then, before the electric door was all the way up, prisoners would be dragged from the wagon, beaten and kicked. When the NBC cameramen were brought in, the policeman said, a lot of officers were cleared from the building to minimize the number of witnesses.

Meanwhile, Julius Boros was taken to the emergency room at Lakeside Hospital by two police officers—one black, one white—who were "very nice to me." There he was examined and X-rayed and given some pills in response to his pleas of pain. Then he was dismissed. "There is nothing wrong with you," he quoted the doctor as saying: "You have some bruises." He was given a prescription to have filled. The two police officers returned Boros to Fifth District headquarters.

Clarence James felt Boros needed further medical attention, and ordered that Boros be taken to the prison ward of Metropolitan General Hospital. Soon thereafter a lawyer from NBC arrived and requested that Boros be taken back to Lakeside Hospital. Evidently the change of plans was conveyed to the police ambulance while Boros was en route to Metropolitan Hospital; he recalls that, during the trip, a policeman (one of the two who had accompanied him on the first trip) opened the window separating front compartment from back and said, "Julius, we just had a call on the radio that changed the story; we are going back to Lakeside."

Boros recalls that he sat at Lakeside Hospital; nothing happened until one of the police officers told him he had to be taken to Central Police Headquarters. Law Director James and Councilman Forbes also went to Central Police Headquarters, only to find that the person in charge in the detective bureau did not have the proper form to release Boros. No one there appeared to know anything about the matter, including a lieutenant who said he had just come on duty; soon thereafter he went home. Eventually, with the help of attorneys for NBC, Boros was released from custody. He was given back his confiscated possessions, but not his camera or his watch.

Boros was then taken to Lutheran Hospital, where he was treated for broken ribs, a ruptured spleen, fractured vertebrae, and facial scrapes. He had bruises and cuts on his face, arms, back, abdomen, and legs. He had a broken tooth. Boros still required hospital treatment after he returned to Chicago August 2.

The police, meanwhile, offered a brief and rectitudinous account of the Boros incident. Patrolman Donald Kupiecki, according to the account, had apprehended a Negro suspect at the corner of 105th and Euclid when he asked Boros to move because he was causing a traffic hazard. According to the *Cleveland Plain Dealer*:

> Kupiecki said that Boros then grabbed his gun from its holster. The two men wrestled for the weapon, which pointed at the policeman, according to the report. When Boros was subdued and was being placed into a police car he kicked Kupiecki, the report states. It adds that Kupiecki was treated at Lakeside Hospital.

Police Prosecutor James Carnes examined both sides of the story and decided that a charge of assault against a policeman was warranted against Boros.[6] He further stated that both cameramen had been treated in a "proper and reasonable" manner by police. In a trial in mid-January 1969, Boros was acquitted of the charges.

(This account of the troubles of Charles Ray and Julius Boros has been based on notarized statements they made in July 1968. During his trial in January 1969, Boros substantially repeated his version of the events and his testimony was corroborated by eyewitnesses. It took the jury only 70 minutes to decide to acquit Boros of the charge of assault and battery. Though Boros' acquittal tends to sustain his account and implies that one or more policemen may have been chargeable with assault, Police Chief Gerity has indicated there will be no departmental investigation of the incidents.)

*   *   *

On Sunday, July 28, Cleveland began to assess the damage from 5 days of violence. A task force of architects and contractors walked through the disturbance area, examining damaged properties, using as their guide a list of 73 properties that had been reported damaged to the police department, the fire department, the mayor's office, or listed as damaged in newspaper accounts. A group of alumni of the Harvard Business School also analyzed the property damage, and in their report to the mayor's office listed damage to 63 separate business establishments. Their list contained 10 fewer names than the task-force report because two of the properties were empty stores with apartments above them damaged by water, four were not privately owned businesses, and four were businesses with two locations, both damaged, but listed only once.

The task force of architects and contractors had surveyed damage and destruction of buildings and estimated the total property loss to be $1,087,505. To this, the Harvard Business School alumni added an estimate of $1,550,225 for losses in equipment and inventory so that, in total, dollar losses exceeded $2.6 million.

Of the 63 business establishments burned or looted, two-thirds were on Superior Avenue. There were 11 damaged businesses on East 105th Street, 10 on St. Clair; the rest were scattered. The damage tended to be clustered. Half of the damaged businesses on Superior Avenue were in a four-block area, between 101st and 105th. In another cluster, between 121st and 124th, 14 businesses were damaged.

Despite the clustering, the damage was far more widespread than during the Hough riots of 1966. Then the burning and looting had been concentrated in a smaller area with only furtive attempts to spread the violence. The unlawful activity in 1968 seemed born of greater self-confidence, less fear of getting caught, than in 1966, and this was interpreted by some as an indication that Mayor Stokes had made a mistake in withdrawing Guardsmen and white policemen.

In defending his policy of withdrawing troops Wednesday night, the mayor admitted that there was property damage, but said he valued life over property. Nonetheless, it would be valuable to know *when* the incidents of property damage took place. Unfortunately, the task force and the Harvard Business School group did not investigate the question, and the only analysis of the timing of looting and arson is one presented by the mayor's office on August 9. According to that analysis, of a total of 47 looting incidents, 26 occurred during the first 24 hours of violence, 17 during the second 24 hours (essentially when the Mayor's Committee was patrolling the streets), and 4 during the remaining days of trouble. Of the 34 fires blamed on vandals and other incendiaries, 14 occurred during the first 24 hours, 7 during the second 24-hour period, and 13 during the rest of the week.

The analysis by the mayor's office would indicate that violent activity had been reduced Wednesday night. The figures, however, do not concur with those presented by others, including a statement published by the *Plain Dealer* on July 26, that "at least forty-seven stores in the cordoned area were either burned or looted yesterday." The precise amount of damage Wednesday night will probably never be confirmed.

Hardest hit among the 63 businesses were groceries (17), furniture stores (10) and clothing stores (8). The Lakeview Tavern, involved in the Tuesday-night shootout, was the only bar reported looted, although the State Liquor Store on East 105th Street was looted twice. (It was not included among the list of 63 damaged establishments, since it is not a privately owned business.) Opinions vary on whether Negro-owned businesses were carefully spared from damage, as they had been during the Hough riots of 1966. A reporter for the *Call & Post* cited evidence that Nergo merchants were spared, though some of the 63 businesses listed are Negro owned. Certainly racial strife was a contributing factor in the pattern of looting and violence. A 20-year-old Negro college student who participated in the violence told an interviewer: "I burned the corner Jew who had been getting my folks for years. I didn't have a desire to loot. I just had to put that cat out of business." But the choice of targets for looting may have had more to do with the commodities coveted than anything else.

The alumni group of the Harvard Business School talked to 50 of the merchants whose businesses had been affected. Of these, only 4 (8 percent) of the owners believed that they had full insurance coverage; 22 (44 percent) had partial insurance coverage; and 24 (48 percent), the largest group, had no insurance coverage at all. At the time of these interviews, 14 of the merchants (28 percent) were open for business and required no help; 20 (40 percent) said they would reopen in the same area if they got short-term financing or adequate insurance payments; seven (14 percent) had not decided what to do; and nine (18 percent) had closed their businesses and did not plan to reopen in the neighborhood.

A. L. Robinson, of the Cleveland Business and Economic Development Corporation, cited an effect of the looting that cannot be measured: "I think the looting put fears in the heart and mind of a great many people who under normal circumstances would like to go into business [in the area]." An older resident of Glenville looked at looted buildings and asked in bitterness: "Why do we destroy ourselves?"

REFERENCES

1. While Jones was facing physical risks, attempting to keep the peace, police were attempting to search for weapons in his apartment. They obtained a search warrant, then called City Hall for permission to enter the cordoned area. According to the *Cleveland Press*, "City Hall called back and told police Jones would give them permission to search his apartment without a warrant. Police declined under those circumstances."

   Wilbur Grattan, another of the active peacekeepers on Wednesday night, had already clashed with the forces of law; the previous night he had been attacked by policemen while attempting to remove a wounded sniper from behind a burning building on Lakeview.

   Three other peacekeepers—George Forbes, Walter Beach, and DeForest Brown—were summoned to a county grand jury hearing on August 24 without the courtesy of prior notification. "To have three policemen come barging into my office with a summons and escort me downtown is an insult," said Councilman Forbes. "No wonder there are riots."

For Harllel Jones there were to be further troubles with the police.

2. The Negro is much better off than he would have you believe, the policeman said. If the truth were known, he added, the Bantus used to sell themselves into slavery because they found it far more advantageous for them to do so. The Bantus, in turn, would take into slavery the Bushmen. The policemen felt the Negroes had been very happy as slaves. When "cotton was king" the times were good and this general propriety of the South extended not only to the whites but also to the Negroes. Now, he felt, Negroes are "con men" trying to convince the American public of how bad things are when really they are not so bad at all.

3. Newspapers quoted Stokes as saying in a 1 a.m. statement that 10 fires had been set by that time Wednesday night. At the City Hall press conference on Aug. 9, Safety Director McManamon stated that, in the 24-hour period beginning at 8:30 p.m., Wednesday evening, there were 23 reported fires, of which only 7 were set by vandals or other incendiaries; the rest were rekindles, false alarms, or fires unrelated to the disturbances. According to McManamon, there were only 17 looting incidents during the 24-hour period.

4. According to one source, Mayor Stokes considered using for nighttime duty only the 400 Guardsmen assigned there during the day. Gen. Del Corso balked at this, insisting that all the troops—more than two thousand—be allowed to patrol the area at night. Del Corso insisted "all or nothing," and Stokes gave in to his wishes.

5. About 2 months later, Harllel Jones had another of his many run-ins with the police (none of which ever ended in a conviction): Police raided the Afro Set on the pretext that missing girls were there. No girls were found, but police confiscated black nationalist flags, marked out-of-town telephone directories, knives, gas masks, and a shotgun. Several days later, 300 Negroes marched in orderly protest over the incident.

On Mar. 3, 1969, Harllel Jones filed a $100,000 damage suit against the three policemen who arrested him in July 1968, charging false arrest and illegal search and seizure.

6. During the early morning hours of July 28, Charles Ray signed a disorderly conduct waiver which effectively immunized him against criminal charges.

Chapter 5

CLEVELAND IN THE AFTERMATH

In the wake of the violence of July 1968, Clevelanders held a mirror to their city. Few were happy with what they saw, but the impressions formed— and the remedies proposed—were many and varied.

Members of the Fraternal Order of Police were angry. Six hundred policemen attended an FOP meeting on August 1 at the Plumbers Union Hall, where heavily armed cops guarded the meeting from the rooftop. There were denunciations of the Stokes administration and a motion, favorably voted, calling for the resignation of Safety Director Joseph McManamon. A similar motion to oust Police Chief Michael Blackwell was defeated, largely out of consideration of his age (67) and longstanding FOP membership. Two nights earlier, a hastily organized meeting of several hundred police wives had also brought denunciations of the Stokes administration.[1]

The mayor refused to fire McManamon. Partly in response to police pressure, however, he and his administration began taking steps to correct longstanding deficiencies in the Police Department. After studying riot control measures in Philadelphia and New York City, the Cleveland police established a 60-man tactical unit, trained in the use of high-powered weapons and prepared to cope with situations involving heavy gunfire. Early in September, Mayor Stokes announced a campaign to recruit 500 additional police officers, and the NAACP began a program to encourage and prepare Negro applicants for the openings. At the same time, the mayor announced a $186,615 grant from the Ford Foundation to be used for police training, to pay tuition costs for policemen enrolled in college courses of their choosing, and to give 900 city employees (including policemen) training in modern management techniques. Other funds came from the U.S. Department of Justice for a new program to improve police-community relations.

More changes were announced. Safety Director McManamon promised to improve the police department's telephone system so that calls could be answered and responded to more quickly and efficiently. Late in September the city began replacing rundown equipment with 164 new police vehicles, and McManamon ordered that patrol cars on the East Side be integrated. Patrick Gerity, who succeeded Michael Blackwell as police chief in mid-October, began a shakeup of the police department that resulted in the reassignment of 104 men.

Some of the changes made police unhappy. When Cleveland's Civil Service Commission expanded the recommended reading for a police promotion test to 26 books—including works on sociology, race relations, and national crime problems—police rebelled. "What are you trying to make us—social workers?"

a policeman asked the secretary of the Civil Service Commission at a meeting of the FOP. Claiming applicants for promotion would not have time to read the books before the exam scheduled for November 16, the FOP sued to have the test delayed and the reading list shortened. The suit was dropped when the Civil Service Commission agreed to reschedule the test for December 14 and reduce the reading list to 14 books.

*   *   *

In an editorial on September 27, the *Cleveland Plain Dealer* called for an end to the tensions and cleavages opened by the Glenville incident.

> This city must not be turned into a mutual aggravation society. It is time for all groups—for their own safety, for their own good, for their children's future—to work together for a peaceable, lawful, orderly community.

The editorial went on to condemn "anyone who tries to keep up the vendetta."

Three days later the *Plain Dealer* began a series of front-page articles, entitled "The Cleveland Police: What's on Their Mind," that effectively kept the vendetta going.

The first installment of the series contained a barrage of quotations from policemen critical of Mayor Stokes, Safety Director McManamon, and Police Chief Blackwell. The article cited pernicious claims that the mayor was "protecting" black nationalists. "He wants to get them in the police department," one officer was quoted. Though it had been promised that the series of articles would separate fact from rumor and myth, the few facts interspersed among the critical opinions were negative ones—for example, concerning outmoded police vehicles. Nothing was said of reforms and improvements then in progress. (The next day, in a side article, the *Plain Dealer* did point out that Cleveland had recently acquired 164 new police vehicles, and that many of these were already in service.)

The second installment, which purported to be about inadequate equipment, opened with a quotation in 14-point type that perhaps unintentionally, had racist overtones: "We're like a British outpost in Africa." Like the first article, the second published comments of policemen alleging lack of leadership and inadequate equipment.

The third installment, on October 2, frankly discussed racial attitudes in the police department. It began with a quotation in large type: "This business about putting a white and Negro policeman in the same car won't work. You got to have a close relationship between partners. If you're not buddies, forget it." There were several quotations of the most-colored-people-appreciate-us sort. Of the troublesome minority of black militants, a police lieutenant offered this analysis: "I think these black nationalists are financed directly by Communists or front groups."

The next installment of "The Cleveland Police: What's on Their Mind" repeated the charge that the mayor was pushing black militants into the police department and contained the allegation that standards were being lowered to let them in. The fifth and last article in the series expressed police dissatisfaction with the courts and with U.S. Supreme Court rulings affecting police procedures.

At the beginning of the series, the *Plain Dealer* had announced that seven reporters—three police reporters, two city hall reporters, (one of them a Negro), and two general assignment reporters—were compiling and writing the series. Nearly all of the work, however, was done by the three police reporters. It has been noted in sociological studies that policemen often develop a conspiratorial outlook on the world and a persecution complex about themselves as a group. ("We're alone, we're a football," a patrolman told one of the reporters.) While police reporters do not necessarily develop the police attitude toward the community, they tend to reflect that attitude as an unconscious or unstated condition of their continuing rapport with the police. "The Cleveland Police: What's on Their Mind" gave free rein to expressions of cynicism, conspiracy, and group paranoia.

The series of articles in the *Plain Dealer* was defensible as "news" because it brought to the attention of Clevelanders serious problems, especially problems of morale, in the police department. It is noteworthy, however, that the police had publicly aired their grievances in the days and weeks following the Glenville incident, that tensions had begun to subside at the time the articles were published (and deserved no rekindling), and that steps had already been taken to improve the situation in the police department. While the series of articles led readers to an impression of a police department suffering stagnation, much of the discontent may actually have stemmed from the uncertainty and insecurity that impending changes and improvements in the department were then creating.

Many Clevelanders who regard the *Plain Dealer* as the city's most responsible newspaper were shocked by the content and tone of "The Cleveland Police: What's on Their Mind." Negro leaders were outraged. The local chapters of the NAACP and CORE announced boycotts against the *Plain Dealer*.

*   *   *

Other articles appearing in the *Cleveland Plain Dealer* fed suspicions that the newspaper was carrying on a vendetta of its own.

On October 3, concurrent with the fourth installment of the police-gripe series, a front-page, five-column headline read: "FBI Is Refused Warrant in Glenville Riot Probe." The article told of the refusal of the U.S. Attorney General in Washington to grant a warrant to the FBI to search a farm in Ashtabula County, 50 miles east of Cleveland, allegedly used by black militants involved in the Glenville incident. A source within the police department was quoted as saying, "Our information was that the FBI felt there were weapons and possibly dead bodies [at the farm]." The implication was made that the Justice Department had thwarted the legitimate work of the FBI, possibly because of racial sensitivities.

According to reporters interviewed for this study, the editors of the *Plain Dealer* had known of the warrant refusal for some time but had saved the story to use as a "tie-in" with the series on police complaints. The *Cleveland Press* investigated the matter and came up with a different story. The *Press* article reported that 50 locations had been reported to Cleveland police as possible gun locations, but there was insufficient information to link the Ashtabula farm with the Glenville shootings. "If we did [have enough information]," a police official said, "we would have sought our own search warrant."

The next day the *Plain Dealer* reported that U.S. Representative William E. Minshall, a Republican running for reelection in a predominantly white suburban area of Cleveland, was calling for a special session of the Federal grand jury to investigate the Glenville incident. Minshall accused U.S. Attorney General Ramsey Clark of "shielding" the guilty parties in the incident. On October 5, the *Plain Dealer*, under an eight-column headline, reported that U.S. Attorney Bernard J. Stuplinski had responded with the promise of a Federal grand jury investigation into the circumstances surrounding the Glenville incident. That afternoon, in the *Cleveland Press*, Stuplinski denied that he had any intention of calling a special Federal grand jury to probe the incident.

> Federal agencies, including the FBI and the Alcohol Tax Unit have been gathering information as to possible violations of Federal law since the first shot was fired in Glenville.

If any violations of Federal law are found, Stuplinski indicated, they would be presented to a regular session of the grand jury.

On October 16, the *Plain Dealer* unleashed a major exposé, revealing details of an incident, embarrassing to the mayor and other high officials, that had taken place 5 months earlier. Under a five-column headline, "CORE 'Bodyguards' Freed by City Hall in Gun Case," the *Plain Dealer* told of the dropping of concealed weapons charges against two Negroes "at the request of unnamed officials at City Hall" in May 1968.

The two East Side Negroes were temporary bodyguards for CORE's former national director, Floyd B. McKissick. They were arrested during the early morning hours of April 5, 8 hours after the assassination of Martin Luther King, outside the home of a prominent Negro stockbroker where McKissick was sleeping. Shortly after they were arrested, Roy Innis, then associate national director of CORE, showed up at Sixth District headquarters to appeal for their release, saying that McKissick had announced on a nationwide newscast that his life had been threatened and that the two arrested men were protecting him. Noting that McKissick had not requested police protection, the officer-in-charge at Sixth District headquarters declined to release the two men. Later in the morning, however, they were released on orders from Chief Prosecutor James S. Carnes.

A jury trial on the concealed weapons charge was scheduled for May 21. On checking the court records on May 16, one of the arresting officers found that the case had been advanced to May 6 and the records marked "Nolle Pros," indicating that the charges had been dropped by Prosecutor Carnes.

After the *Plain Dealer* revelations on October 16, John T. Corrigan, prosecutor of Cuyahoga County, proceeded to take over the case dropped by the city of Cleveland, an unusual move considering the charges were only for a misdemeanor. Corrigan succeeded in getting indictments against the two men from the county grand jury. Carnes, who had resigned as city prosecutor in September, was unresponsive to reporters' questions about the case. Mayor Stokes at first refused to comment on the case, then admitted he had been instrumental in having the charges dropped. But he defended the move as necessary during the volatile hours following the King assassination, when "we were . . . trying to hold the city together and trying to keep down any issues that might erupt."

That seemed a reasonable explanation to many Clevelanders, and reason enough for allowing the issue to die quietly. Reporters interviewed for this study indicated that the editors of the *Plain Dealer* had knowledge of the dropped charges months before they decided to publish their exposé.

*   *   *

The *Plain Dealer* articles, opening old wounds, suggesting conspiracies, casting doubt on the integrity of the Stokes administration, may have increased the credibility of a racist pamphlet widely distributed in the white neighborhoods of Cleveland's West Side. Entitled "Warning!," the bulletin detailed an alleged plot by black nationalists to attack the West Side to "get the white man where he lives." Weapons and ammunition for the attack, it said, had recently been moved from a farm in Ashtabula County. The plot would include planned auto accidents to block streets, fire bombings in a concentrated area to draw police into an ambush, and a main attack by 50 to 75 carloads of black nationalists, shooting at every white person in sight as they rampaged through the West Side and escaped through the western suburbs.

The warning was built upon distrust of the Stokes administration. The anonymous authors said they had warned the Cleveland police of the plot, but the police has replied that "with this administration they probably won't be allowed to take any action." Because the black militants have a friend in City Hall, the pamphlet said, they are better equipped and organized than they were in July. "Because we can expect no preventive action or help from Cleveland City Hall, it has become necessary for you, the potential victim, to protect yourself and your property."

Others were busy during the fall of 1968 polarizing the Cleveland community in other ways. Robert Annable, a telephone company employee and the president of the United Citizens Council in Cleveland, organized a rightwing group called the Citizens Committee for Law Enforcement. The purpose of the new organization was to back police in their demands for heavy weaponry, to provide financial support to policemen in civil suits and disciplinary actions, to "investigate" the liberal organizations that were pressing for investigation of the police department, and to set into motion a campaign to have Mayor Stokes removed from office. At the end of September, Roy Richards, head of the new group and chairman of the Cleveland branch of the Wallace for President Committee, filed a recall petition in probate court, stating that Stokes had acted illegally "in allegedly channeling 'Cleveland: Now!' funds to Negro militant groups, allegedly appearing at a public function with armed black nationalists, and allegedly mishandling the restoration of order during the Glenville disorders last July."

The Citizens Committee for Law Enforcement also printed up posters portraying Mayor Stokes and Safety Director McManamon, with the caption, "WANTED to answer questions for the murder of three policemen." The poster began showing up on bulletin boards in police stations, alongside another which showed Mayor Stokes marching in a parade on the anniversary of the Hough riots behind armed black nationalists and captioned, "These pictures show how to start a riot which KILLS, wounds and maims policemen who are replaced by BLACK POWER social workers by the Mayor."

Through the fall of 1968, white residents of Cleveland's West Side who put credence in rumors and anonymous pamphlets waited fruitlessly for an invasion by black nationalists. What came instead were further instances of polarization, instigated by the anonymous pamphlets and several racially oriented beatings on Cleveland's West Side. A rumor spread among parents of white students at Shuler Junior High School and John Marshall High School that their children were threatened with mass attacks by black nationalists called in by Negro students to protect them. Negro parents were told that white gangs were assembling to attack Negro students. On Monday, October 21, 70 Negro students walked out of John Marshall High School and a smaller number walked out of Shuler Junior High School. Amidst this walkout, rumors spread over the West Side that students and principals had been beaten up.

Negro groups contributed to Cleveland's polarization. In September, noisy interference of a City Council meeting by black militants did little to win sympathy for their grievances, however meritorious. And in October it was revealed that a group of black nationalists calling themselves the Black Information Service were attempting to coerce some East Side merchants into turning over 10 percent of their profits, allegedly for neighborhood-improvement projects. The extortion shamed the Negro community and brought condemnation from its leaders.

*   *   *

Many months after the violence of July 1968, the neighborhood of Glenville bore the scars. On Lakeview Road there was a large vacant area where two houses burned to the ground during the gun battle, giving the block the appearance of a row of teeth with two incisors missing. On Superior Avenue there were stores that were black, gaping shells, others that hid protectively behind plywood panels at their windows. Graffiti scrawled on the plywood told of hatred and smoldering violence. "Black people buy Protection: 20-20 shotguns Passport to freedom" was scribbled on a boarded-up drycleaning store. Said another: "Kill Wild Beast. Stand and be counted in the war against the Beast." Here and there were more positive evidences of the new black pride. The marquee of an old movie theater that had become Muhammad's Mosque proclaimed: "Allah is the Greatest." Among the stores doing business on the avenue a number bore Muslim names, some incongruously: The Shabazz Market advertised kosher meat. Some stores sold African handicrafts, as Ahmed once had done.

Though they had cause for bitterness and fear, many merchants elected to stay on in Glenville. One who had particular cause for bitterness was Jack Friedman, owner of a department store at East 105th and Superior. Friedman had been active in the community affairs of Glenville, a white man seeking racial harmony and better conditions for Negroes of the neighborhood. Most of his employees, including several top managers, were black. Friedman made many of them stockholders in the enterprise. A Negro businessman said to him once, "Friedman, why don't you put on burnt coffee? You're one of us." During the Hough riots of 1966, Friedman's store had been spared while others nearby had windows smashed.

In 1968, his department store was hit on the first night of violence, some time after Friedman had returned home from a meeting at the Office of Economic Opportunity. It was "like the feeling of cold ice," he recalls, when he learned of the damage. The store was a shambles. Display cases were smashed, their contents gone. Vandals broke into a case displaying shoes only to discover that all the shoes were for right feet. Looters grabbed clothes even from the mannequins, sometimes taking pajama bottoms and leaving the tops. Friedman estimates that, of $60,000 worth of merchandise in stock, he was left with less than $500 worth.

But Friedman decided to stay. "I have faith in Glenville and a small bunch of hoodlums isn't going to destroy my faith in it." He wanted to help heal the wounds and continue to work for the betterment of the Negro community. "I happen to be of a minority group myself," he said. "I know what they've gone through."

REFERENCE

1. A police sergeant, Louis Bors, took matters into his own hands 2 weeks later. He went to the Governor's office in Columbus (wearing his uniform), carrying a 10-page petition calling for the ouster of Stokes, McManamon, and Law Director James for "willfully neglecting to enforce the law, gross neglect of duty, malfeasance, misfeasance, and non-feasance in office." Governor Rhodes refused to act on the petition

Chapter 6

A NEW PATTERN?

In recent years America has seemed embarked on a course in which outbreaks of racial violence deepen the rift between black and white, and the rising tensions and mutual distrust that lead to further outbreaks of violence. The pernicious cycle cannot be broken, obviously enough, until tensions are defused and mutual trust is established.

Racial violence in the United States has a long history, and the changing patterns of that violence have reflected changes in the relationships and attitudes between blacks and whites. Slavery in the 18th century established master and slave in the relationship of dominant and subservient, and violence was a legitimate means for the white master to underscore and enforce that relationship. As Gunnar Myrdal noted in *An American Dilemma* (1944):

> The social pattern of subduing the Negroes by means of physical force was inherent in the slavery system. The master himself, with the backing, if needed, of the local police and, indeed, of all white neighbors, had to execute this force, and he was left practically unrestricted by any formal laws.

Negroes did not always resign themselves to this subjugation, and there were several notable attempts at slave rebellion. All of these attempts failed, but the mere fact that they had been tried served to increase the legitimacy of white-inflicted violence for maintaining slaves in subjugation.

With emancipation the pattern of violence changed. Vigilante justice, especially in the form of lynching, was an extralegal means of inflicting punishment on whites as well as blacks, but increasingly it became, especially in the South, a mode for keeping Negroes "in line." The Tuskegee Institute, which began counting lynchings in 1882, established four criteria for including events in their records:

1. There must be legal evidence that a person was killed.
2. The person must have met death illegally.
3. A group must have participated in the killing.
4. The group must have acted under the pretext of service to justice, race, or tradition.

In the peak year of 1892, the Tuskegee Institute counted 161 lynchings of Negroes, declining to 67 in 1910 and 20 in 1930. In 1963, the Institute stopped counting, for lynching as a mode of racial violence had virtually disappeared, and the count no longer provided a useful index to race relations.

Another pattern emerged late in the 19th century: riots, in which whites were the attackers, Negroes the victims. Generally whites sought to inflict personal injury on a group of Negroes; the Negroes, as victims, usually did little to counterattack. In 1908, the white community of Springfield, Ill., enraged by two alleged rapes of white women by Negroes, launched 2 days of rioting, burning, and lynching aimed at the Negro residents of the city. Most Negroes fled in terror. About 2,000 of them gathered for protection in the Springfield Arsenal; others fled to safety elsewhere. Before the riot ended, 5,000 militia were patrolling the streets of Springfield. Riots of a similar sort occurred in Wilmington, N.C. (1896); East St. Louis, Ill. (1917); Washington, D.C. (1919); and Tulsa, Okla. (1921).

Negroes did not remain passive in rioting. The next pattern to emerge was one in which the opposing races sought to inflict physical harm on each other. An example was the 1919 riot in Chicago. On July 27 of that year, a 17-year-old Negro drowned during an interracial scuffle at a public beach in Chicago. The incident touched off a week of racial warfare. Though the riot produced property damage, the major objective was physical harm. Thirty-eight persons were reported killed (23 Negroes and 15 whites), while a reported total of 537 were injured (342 Negroes, 178 whites, 17 undetermined). Even with National Guard units in the city, the violence did not die down until Chicago faced rain and falling temperatures. The same type of racial violence was evident in the 1943 riot in Detroit, Mich. There, in less than 3 full days of rioting, 710 individuals were injured or killed. Once again, persons of both races participated in the violence; the major form of violence was physical attack.

The spate of riots in American cities during the mid-1960's followed a different pattern. These were Negro-dominated, property-oriented riots. Negroes initiated the violence and directed their hostilities toward property rather than persons. Most of the property was white owned but located within the Negro ghetto. The violence seldom spread beyond the borders of the ghetto. Generally the only white casualties of the violence were police or other law enforcement officers trying to control the rioting.

The precedent for this kind of violence occurred in Harlem in 1935. On March 19, a Negro youth was caught stealing from a dimestore in that predominantly Negro section of New York. A crowd that gathered outside the store got the impression that the boy had been murdered by white employees of the store. As the rumor spread, Negro mobs began to roam the streets of Harlem, breaking store windows and looting. Except for confrontations between police and looters, almost no whites were drawn into the violence. Looting continued through the next day, but was finally brought under control by police and local Negro leaders.

In 1967, riots of this pattern occurred in a number of American cities. The National Advisory Commission on Civil Disorders (Kerner Commission) studied these riots and concluded:

> While the civil disorders of 1967 were racial in character, they were not *inter*racial. The 1967 disorders, as well as earlier disorders of the recent period, involved action within Negro neighborhoods against symbols of American society—authority and property—rather than against white persons.

*   *   *

The violence that erupted in Cleveland at the end of July 1968 may have marked the beginning of a new pattern. Though it soon fell into the established pattern of Negroes destroying property in the ghetto, it began as violence aimed at personal injury. Black dominated throughout, it ended in more white casualties than black. Though the white victims were policemen, attacked as symbols of the white society rather than as men, the mode of vengeance had taken a significant step beyond damage to white-owned businesses. A small, well-equipped army of black extremists was responsible for the bloodshed (whether or not they fired the first shot). The depths of anger and extreme beliefs from which the violence spring are indicated by the fact that the presence of a Negro in the mayor's chair did not prevent it from happening. The extent of alienation of many blacks from the white society is indicated by the fact that Negro leaders could not stop the violence once it started. (A fair appraisal of the mayor's one-night strategy would acknowledge that no blood was shed, that the peace patrols were undermanned, that most of the trouble came from juveniles, and that traditional methods of full-scale repression during riots have not been notably successful either.)

To acknowledge that the Cleveland riots began as person-oriented violence is not to say that the Glenville incident was a planned ambush, part of an intercity conspiracy, or "the first stage of revolutionary armed struggle," as Phil Hutchings of the Student Nonviolent Coordinating Committee called it. On the same day that Hutchings gave his interpretation of the event, U.S. Attorney General Ramsey Clark offered the opinion that the Glenville incident was "the random act of a handful of very extreme and violence-prone militants." He found "even less evidence now of militant agitation or conspiratorial efforts to cause . . . [riots] than in the past several years." Mayor Stokes also concluded there was no evidence of a police ambush or intercity plot. He blamed the incident on the "spontaneous action taken by a group who were armed and emotionally prepared to do violence." After its investigations the Cuyahoga County grand jury "substantially" agreed with the mayor's analysis.

Baxter Hill had a convincing rejoinder to the conspiracy theory. "When an insurrection comes," he said, "everybody'll be in it and we'll all know about it."

It is beyond the scope of this inquiry to speculate whether such an insurrection, in Cleveland or elsewhere, will ever come. But, like the specter of an atomic holocaust that now forces nations to seek peace among themselves, the possibility of interracial civil war may yet goad Americans, black and white, to noble steps: to erase tensions and misunderstandings, to correct longstanding inequities, to restore tranquillity in their nation.

THE TRIAL AND CONVICTION OF FRED (AHMED) EVANS

Last August, the grand jury of Cuyahoga County met and returned seven first-degree murder indictments against Fred (Ahmed) Evans. On March 6, 1969, the seven counts were amended at the request of counsel for the defense to delete the word "murder" which is a conclusion and insert "to kill by shooting" in its place.

Counts 1, 3, 5, and 7 pertain to the killing of Leroy C. Jones, Louis E. Golonka, Willard J. Wolff, and James E. Chapman as civilians and read as follows:

> ... unlawfully, purposely, and of deliberate and premeditated malice, did kill one [Jones, Golonka, Wolff, Chapman] by shooting him, pursuant to a conspiracy to kill and murder theretofore entered into by and between the said Fred (Ahmed) Evans, Lathan Donald, Alfred Thomas, John Hardwick and Leslie Jackson.

Counts 2, 4, and 6 pertain to the killing of Leroy C. Jones, Louis E. Golonka, and Willard J. Wolff while in the discharge of their duties as policemen and read as follows: "... unlawfully, purposely and wilfully did kill [Jones, Golonka, Wolff] a duly appointed, qualified and acting policeman of the City of Cleveland, County of Cuyahoga, in pursuance of a conspiracy to kill, while said [Jones, Golonka, Wolff] was in the discharge of his duties as a policeman."

The criminal statutes in Ohio upon which these indictments are based are 2901.01 and 2901.04. They respectively read as follows:

Conspiracy

> One who enters into a conspiracy to commit an unlawful act is guilty of any unlawful act of his co-conspirators in furtherance of the conspiracy and it is not necessary that the conspiracy be one to commit the identical offense charged in the indictment or even a similar one, it being enough that the offense charged was one which might have been contemplated as the result of the conspiracy, and it is not in error for the court to so charge under an indictment for first degree murder where a conspiracy to rob has been shown.

Killing of a Police Officer

No person shall purposely and willfully kill a sheriff, deputy sheriff, constable, policeman, or marshall while such sheriff, deputy sheriff, constable, policeman, or marshall is in the discharge of his duties.

Whoever violates this section is guilty of murder in the first degree and shall be punished by death unless the jury trying the accused recommends mercy, in which case the punishment shall be imprisonment for life.

The State introduced 266 exhibits and called 86 witnesses in order to prove circumstantially, if not conclusively, that Ahmed Evans with four other co-defendants was guilty of conspiring to murder on July 23, 1968. The State built its case on the testimony of approximately eight gun dealers who sold guns to Ahmed, and the testimony of Robert Boone, a neighbor, who said that he saw cars with out-of-State license plates delivering guns to Ahmed's house. The prosecution demonstrated that Ahmed had the funds necessary to make these purchases by calling DeForest Brown, director of the Hough Development Corporation, who testified that Ahmed's group had received a grant from "Cleveland: Now."

Later they brought in Detective Robert Birt, who gathered many of the guns and bullets from Ahmed's apartment and the scene of the shootings on the night of the 23d. Sgt. Victor Kovacic was asked to present his findings regarding the matching of bullets and guns to wounds. During the progress of the trial, the State offered into evidence a slug fired from Ahmed's gun which was allegedly found in police Car 591.

Several key witnesses were also called upon to relate their contacts with the defendant. Walter Washington, a youth who claimed that he was at 12312 Auburndale on the morning of July 23, stated that he heard Ahmed talk about killing "the beast" and said that Ahmed showed his followers how to use the guns present in the house at that time. Patrolman James O'Malley and several other police officers from the surveillance teams assigned to watch 12312 testified that Ahmed left 12312 Auburndale with other men, armed, at about 8:10 p.m. on July 23. Another crucial identification of Ahmed was made by William McMillan, the tow-truck driver, who was shot and who alleged that it was Ahmed who shot him. Finally Sgt. John Ungvary related conversations he had with Ahmed wherein Ahmed described his brand of black nationalism as "revolution by force." He also stated that Ahmed predicted "blood in the streets of Cleveland" and a war by the black people on "the beast."

The defense emphasized that the corner's examination revealed that two of the policemen, Golonka and Wolff, were legally drunk at the time of death. According to the eminent forensic pathologist, Dr. Cyril Wecht, James Chapman was killed by a gun held at no more than 6 inches from his head—and hence by a policeman. The defense maintained that the guns in the possession of Ahmed's group were bought to form a rifle club and that they were legal, legitimate purchases. They disputed the credibility of Walter Washington as a witness (he was a convicted arsonist and thief). Several witnesses wh were at the hospital when McMillan was admitted testified that McMillan reported that he did not see who shot him.

Reports were presented to the jury that Car 591 has been repaired in September 1968, and that there had been no detection of a bullet imbedded in the vehicle until April 1969. In order to impugn the validity of police testimony, the defense subpenaed seven persons who testified that they were victims of police brutality at the Lakeview Tavern on July 23. No policemen admitted having knowledge of these acts. A key defense witness was Joseph Turpin, Jr., a workhouse guard in whose house Ahmed surrendered. He claimed that Ahmed was in his house from 20 minutes after the shooting began until he surrendered to the police. He said that Ahmed was not one of the men he saw shooting at the tow-truck driver and that Ahmed had said he wanted to surrender to stop the shooting and burning.

After the closing statements by lawyers of both the State and defense, Judge George J. McMonagle explained the charge of the law to the jury. He told the jury that the indictment was not evidence in the guilt of the defendant. It was merely a formal way of legally charging a person with a crime. In actuality, a presumption of innocence must surround the defendant until the jury comes to a verdict. Regarding the use of a "reasonable doubt," Judge McMonagle stated that it must be more than a possible or imaginary doubt. A reasonable doubt is when the jury cannot "feel an abiding conviction to a moral certainty of the truth of the charge." He told the jury that they also must determine the degree of credibility that they would assign each witness.

In further explaining the charge of aiding and abetting, he cited Revised Code Sec. 1.17 which states that to aid or abet is "to help or assist . . . encourage, counsel or incite. To procure one to do something is to persuade, to induce, to prevail upon or cause it to be done."

His definition of conspiracy was a paraphrasing of conspiracy as it appears in 2901.01 of the Ohio Revised Code. In McMonagle's words, a "conspiracy is merely an agreement or understanding between the parties to the conspiracy. It need not be an expressed agreement. . . . It may be implied from all of the evidence and circumstances . . ."[1]

He charged that "direct testimony of conspiracy is unnecessary, but it [the conspiracy] may be established by circumstantial evidence showing concerted action in committing an unlawful act, or by proof of facts creating an inference or inferences that the unlawful act was in furtherance of a conspiracy." The judge said that if circumstantial evidence is consistent with either guilt or innocence, the jury must give the defendant the benefit of the doubt. The jury may draw inferences from proven facts but not inferences upon inferences.

He informed them that the defendant was innocent if the State had not proven beyond a reasonable doubt these charges. On the other hand, if the defendant was found to be guilty of any one of the charges of first degree murder, the jury still had the option of granting or withholding mercy.

One of the final parts of Judge McMonagle's charge to the jury was that of the lesser but included charges: murder in the second degree and voluntary and involuntary manslaughter.

The jury retired to deliberate immediately after the judge's charge at about 4 p.m., Saturday, May 10, 1969. They discussed the evidence for the remainder of the day. On Sunday, the jurors took several oral ballots and eight written ones—seven for the seven counts and one for mercy. By the end of the day all the jurors agreed to the defendant's guilt, but one juror wanted more time to think about the issue of mercy which she alone at that point favored.

When the jurors reconvened on Monday morning, May 12, they were unanimous that Ahmed was guilty of first-degree murder on all seven counts, without mercy. On that Monday, approximately at noon, the verdict was returned in open court.

Before sentencing Ahmed, the judge asked him if he had any statements. Ahmed replied:

> I fully understand the ways of life as they are now, and the truth of the matter is I have no regret. . . . I have no malice towards anyone, white people nor anyone else . . . .
>
> This will not end by the means that have been used today against the black man who are willing, who are able, who are strong enough to stand up.
>
> The electric chair or fear of anything won't stop the black man of today.
>
> I feel justified in that I did the best I could. And, of course, concerning these charges I am not a murderer.

Judge McMonagle answered:

> . . . If it can be said there was any defense you presented . . . it was that you did not agree with our laws, and apparently you were not bound by them. . . .
>
> I think it is perfectly obvious that we cannot have a system where every man is his own law.

Furthermore, Ahmed had inflicted a horrible wound on the community. The judge hoped that the community, white and black together, would continue to work together for coequal status within the law.

Thereupon, he sentenced Ahmed to die in the electric chair on September 22, 1969, between the hours of midnight and sunrise.

REFERENCE

1. The essence of a conspiracy is the agreement or joining together, and in some States and under Federal law, this combination for an unlawful end is itself a crime, even though the agreed act is never carried out. In Ohio, however, conspiracy is not unlawful per se, and there can be no violation of the law unless some substantive crime (here, murder) is committed pursuant to the conspiracy. Even then, the defendant is charged and tried for the substantive offense, not for the conspiracy.